Lemon
A Memoir

First Edition, Second Printing

ISBN: 979-8-218-73270-7 (Paperback)

www.stephenkubacki.com

For my wife, Wendy, who listened to these stories
before I had the guts to write them down.

One

I grew up playing in the headwater creeks of the Pinnebog River. I played in those drains, especially the ditch behind my house, almost every day. Things happened there.

I learned to forget, I vaguely remember now.

We were hanging out in the tree fort. He entered and joined our child's play. Something made a bright snap and a quick flash of silver.

Afterward, he grinned and slithered away like a snake. I was too naïve to understand and too young to stop him.

My great grandma Adelaide nearly died as an infant. She was born in 1894 long before there was medical equipment to help premature babies. There wasn't much that could be done except pray for the sick little elf.

Farmers can be stubborn and never give up especially in desperate situations. Her family swaddled Adelaide with a small blanket and improvised a cradle by laying her in a small wooden crate. To incubate the sick baby, they set the crate on top of their wood burning stove, the door propped open, a fire burning low. Little Ada stayed hydrated and nourished, without intravenous saline or a feeding tube, with any milk they could get. At first, the family used their fingertips, and later, an eye dropper to feed her. Mom told me they blended breast milk, cow's milk, and some Karo corn syrup for extra calories.

The last week of May 1968 Mom was near the end of pregnancy with her belly ready to burst. I did the math. I was conceived two weeks after Mom and Dad got married in August 1967. They wanted it – the sex of their baby – to be a surprise. Blue or pink, pink or blue, any color clothes will do. Because the pregnancy was making *her* feel a bit blue, one of Dad's older sisters, Nina, came to see Mom. In an attempt to improve Mom's mood, the ladies went for a short drive in Verona near the Kubacki farm. They rolled up and down the glacial cut hills breathing in the heavy countryside pollen, watching the wheat billow in the breeze, as Aunt Nina encouraged Mom about her new role as a mom. After I was born, Dad asked Nina and her husband, Rusty, to be my Godparents.

While Dad was in the Army Reserves, the old man bought a Plymouth and a tiny prefab house on the middle block of South Street in Bad Axe. He paid for it with cash from the Army and loans from the bank. When Dad showed his parents the shiny black Satellite, Grandpa Kubacki asked him if there was a note on the car. Dad said he had taken out a loan on the house and the car. Grandpa K looked at him through his bushy eyebrows with a mild glare.

"Why did you get a loan, Buckley?"

"I couldn't wait to ask for your help."

"Go outside and get the jar."

Dad retrieved a wide mouth canning jar from the hollow box elder tree and brought it inside. Grandpa peeled several thousand dollars from the wad in the jar and handed it to Dad. The cache of money looked no smaller than before the gift. Because of Grandpa's generosity Dad paid off the car and had some money to pay down the principal on the house.

Their new home was a boxy ranch when they bought it. Dad put on an addition and laid a patio a few years after they moved in. Other than excavating the lot and laying blocks for a crawl space he did the work himself. In our family photo album, there's a picture of Dad wearing a three-pocket cloth apron filled with nails, a hammer in his hand, *and I'm helping him.* He turned the old kitchen into a dining room with a snack bar. Built a new kitchen, a family room, and a master bedroom on top of the fresh plywood floor which still smelled like wood glue from the mill. Covered the walls of the living room and bedroom with dark brown sheets of wood paneling. Laid down a vivid, multi-colored, striped carpeting in the den, and a green and gold patterned carpet in the kitchen and dining room. The last improvement he made, so the entire town could see who was in charge now, was painting a large, dark blue K on the garage centered in the sixteen panels of the heavy, solid wood, manually operated door.

On the big day when Mom went into labor, Dad drove her to the hospital. The nurses wheeled her into the delivery room while Dad paced back and forth in the waiting room of the Harbor Beach hospital. I was born on June 1, 1968.

Soon after I was born, Mom returned to work. Since there wasn't a lot of time to breastfeed, she pumped milk with one of those cumbersome contraptions. Because her job schedule had gotten too hectic and the machine probably didn't feel comfortable anyway, she weaned me off breast milk and started me on formula. *I did not like it.*

Grandma Booms suggested Mom should mix unpasteurized cow's milk from the dairy farm with the formula. She told Mom what her mom, Little Ada, had gone through and they decided to try the milk and Karo syrup recipe with me. It must've worked because I was a chubby baby in my first professional portrait, leaning on the back of a lounge chair covered with a gray cloth that looked like an old window curtain. For years I wondered why my parents had dressed me like a girl for the picture because the straps of my pull up pants had aligned with the gray drapery to create a perfect illusion of me wearing a dress.

Mom was one of the older kids in a huge family of fifteen children. Because the family was so large my mom always had younger siblings to watch and toddlers needing constant diaper changes. As a new mom she already knew what to do when I came into the world.

While baby-sitting me Aunt Nina was showing her daughters basic child care techniques when Mom arrived at Zajac's after work. They were helping to clean me up and learn how to change a diaper.

A lot of people said, "Rusty must be blessed because God gave him all daughters." And other people said, "Poor Rusty, he's got nothing but girls."

In the evening while smoking pipes he filled the entire house with sweet tobacco smoke. He was a modest man who wore pajamas, a robe, and slippers in the evening – unlike my old man who wore nothing but a towel around his waist after a bath and tighty whities for sleepwear.

Uncle Rusty's girls must've been intrigued by the presence of male genitalia. They were looking down at me while I looked up at them when something happened. I can only imagine what was going through the young girls' minds. They must've been fascinated by my nudity because my cousins, Melissa and all her sisters, were giggling and pointing at my penis when one of them reached down and gave it a few good yanks!

Mom said *something like this,* "Your cousin's a boy. Boys have a pee-pee down there not a *ciuściuś* like you girls."

Soon afterward, my parents found a lady to sit with me at home. One day Mom got out of work early and being excited to see her new baby boy she drove straight home. After coming into the house, she lifted me from a pile of blankets on the floor, held me in her arms, and gave me a warm hug. After a bit of small talk, Mom paid the babysitter and said goodbye.

When she had first got home and picked me up, she noticed a *package* in my drawers and probably thought, *Steve just made a b.m. The new sitter didn't have a chance to change him yet. I got this.*

After taking me to the bedroom, Mom laid me down and removed my rubber pants and soiled cloth diaper. She gasped and said, "What did she do to you?

Oh, heck," because my diaper was full of shit from the entire day. I'm not sure how long the woman had babysat for me, but after dinner and cleaning up the evening slop Mom called the sitter and fired the bitch over the phone.

My earliest memory is of when I was three years old. My baby sister, Wren, was with us. She is the first person I remember meeting. Wren was born in 1972, two years after me. I was no longer alone, I had a sister, a friend.

Dad was driving the blue Fury to Grandma Booms's house for Sunday dinner while Mom sat next to him holding Wren in her lap. I was sitting in the car seat, a clunky, folding contraption. A one-size-fits-all safety engineering marvel. Mom and Dad were staring out the windshield looking down Huron Avenue as I stared out the side window. Something caught my attention. I made sense of the sign and said, "Ed is on," as we drove past a low gray building.

Mom looked out the window at the electric company office, turned toward Dad, and said, "I didn't know he could do that. Ed is on. Edison. Detroit Edison. He read the sign, dear."

"Are you kidding me, Charlie?"

"No, I'm not kidding, Buckley. He read the sign."

"Well, *Matka Boska!* The little shit can read."

Mrs. Bert was my favorite babysitter because she made the best grilled cheese sandwiches in the world. She made them with two slices of Wonder bread, plenty of real butter, and Velveeta cheese which oozed from the edges of the fried sandwich.

She had a litter of puppies to give away and gave one of the pups to me. The scruffy, black and white puppy looks as big as a horse standing next to me in an old photograph. I'm beaming with joy. The picture and my vague memory of the puppy are the only evidence it existed. Was it a boy dog or girl dog? I don't know. Nobody seems to know. No one remembers.

The lovable little thing surely felt abandoned outside by itself at night. It spent the whole night, for three nights, howling in the garage. Mom didn't understand why it made such a racket. Their dogs didn't make that much noise at home on the farm.

Of course, you know I don't remember a word of it, but Mom said, "Cricket is keeping everybody in the neighborhood awake. We have to take the puppy back to Mrs. Bert. Dogs belong on a farm." I think Mom was the only one it kept up at night. I don't think a single neighbor had complained about the noise.

For a long time afterward, until you were seven or eight, another dog haunted you at night when you couldn't fall asleep. As cars drove down the street a puppy materialized in the center of the living room and walked towards the hallway. The dog padded along between the lines of light and shadow made by a passing car's headlights. The dog from the Probus painting in the living room came alive, left the boy and his fishing pole near the tiny waterfall, climbed out of that world, and leaped into this one. The puppy trotted into the hallway right up to the edge of your doorway, looked at you, and then disappeared into the dark shadows at the foot of the bed.

Grandma Kubacki raised geraniums in a sunroom on the south side of her seldom painted house. She could take a small stem and leaf, place the cutting in an empty margarine tub filled with moist soil, and after waiting a couple of weeks, roots sprouted from her clipping. The Kubacki farmhouse, which sat on top of a big hill, was a large two-story, chunky box with a full front porch spanning from one edge of the house to the other. In the lawn were two rough-hewn Adirondack chairs, probably made by Grandpa. A rotary mower sat in the partially cut, long, thick grass. Grandma's apple trees – one with four varieties grafted by her onto one trunk. The deep basement was open except for a support post in the center of the large room. A wringer washer and washtubs stood in one corner. In the opposite corner sat an enormous pile of wood, neatly stacked and arranged by my petite grandma, waiting to be fed into their large coal and wood burning furnace.

Lucy and Aloysious Kubacki raised twelve kids in that big old farmhouse. They lost one of them, my Aunt Helen, at six years old from complications due to multiple congenital birth defects. They also lost a son, less than a year old, but reused the child's name for their next born son. This practice, to honor a lost child, was once fairly common.

Grandma Booms was named for a sister born immediately before her. The first Florence Cecelia, my great aunt, only lived a few months – but the second

Florence Cecelia, my grandma, lived a long hearty life. Grandma often told us she didn't want to be named after her dead sister.

Because my dad was the second youngest of the family brood with only Aunt Lily behind him, he wasn't allowed to help his older brothers feeding and milking the cows in the barn or help with fall harvests in the field. I'm sure that's why Dad developed a taste for *women's work* – that's what he called it – such as cooking and sewing. Dad always loved improvising recipes. When a certain ingredient wasn't in our cupboards, he substituted it with something we did have on hand. When someone complimented him on his improvised recipe, he usually couldn't remember what he had used and would tell them, "I used a little of this and a little of that."

Grandma Kubacki always carried a Rosary with her and prayed over the beads at least once a day. *Hail Mary, full of grace, the Lord is with thee.* She attended Mass whenever possible, sometimes seven days a week. On holidays, funerals, and other special occasions Lucy handed out shots of ginger brandy to everybody and often took a sip for herself. *Blessed art thou among women, and blessed is the fruit of thy womb, Jesus.*

I don't remember eating anything she cooked but she always had interesting food in her icebox like pickled eggs, pickled bologna, homemade horseradish, and duck blood soup. Things which I never tried because I was too finicky. As a kid, I was completely grossed out by *gołąbki*. Adults encouraged me to try the savory stuffed cabbage. They called it pigs in a blanket even though it contained no pork. Grandma K made it with ground beef, rice, and home canned tomato sauce. *Hail Mary,* Matka Boska, *pray for us sinners now and at the hour of our deaths. Amen.* I was eighteen when she died. Her funeral procession was two and a half miles long.

Grandma Kubacki never learned to drive. Aunt Lily once said, "Mom wished she'd learned to drive so she could leave the house and get away from Grandpa." Grandma was probably intimidated by her husband like us grandkids were. He scared the shit out all of us younger kids and my older cousins were scared of him too. I'd bet all forty-nine of his grandchildren were scared of him! Grandpa had large, overgrown, bushy eyebrows that made him look scary, and for a short man, he was a big, intimidating guy. When Aloysious cleaned up and put on a suit, he looked dangerous, like a gangster, with his wife, a flapper moll, at his side. We often saw him stomping around the house angry about something. I can see why Grandma might have wanted to leave the house and go for a drive around the country mile while he cooled off. But I think she also desired his protection and ensured her dependence on her tough husband by never learning to drive.

On his farm, Grandpa raised potatoes for the table, grain for market, and alfalfa hay for his cows. A string of small garages housed his modest tractor, plow, harrow, and other farm implements. Grandpa K used to play Polkas on an old beat-up fiddle. My cousin, Rodney Zajac, and I, pretending to be raucous rock stars, smashed it one day while playing air guitar. But because it was already beat up, uncared for, and hadn't had strings for several years, Grandpa shrugged it off and didn't even scold us. He drove a black V-8 Maverick. It reeked of ammonia because he was getting old and pissed his pants all the time. The smell of urine mixed and mingled with the funky smell of tobacco chaw and spit. He chewed tobacco in the car *and in the house.* Grandma kept a plastic runner under his gallon milk jug with the top cut off to keep the tobacco juice and spit off her hand made braided rugs.

"Be careful, don't trip on *Dziadzo's* jug!"

One early spring day, on a cold, sunny afternoon, the Zajac girls had taken Grandma K grocery shopping at the closest store ten miles away in Bad Axe. I had tagged along with them. Taking *Busia* back to her house we hit a thin patch of ice on Verona Road. My cousin Melissa was trying hard to handle the black ice but the car suddenly spun-out of control and she put the Mustang halfway in a ditch. Melissa eventually got the car back on the road, reassured my startled grandma, and continued to the farm.

At the farmhouse, we were watching old reruns on a black and white TV with rabbit ears when all of a sudden, the unpredictable spring weather changed and a lightning bolt cracked out of the sky. It started pouring rain. We all ran to the window for a better view of the storm. We saw Aloysious galloping up the driveway from the barn with a slop pail. He didn't come into the house but ran into the fallow field west of the driveway.

One of my cousin's said, "What's Grandpa doing out there?"

"Yeah, what's he doing, Grandma?"

Aunt Nina said, "He's blessing the thunderstorm."

"Aloyzi blesses the first thunderstorm every spring," Grandma said, "so we have good crops."

We watched as Grandpa dipped a small broom, his homemade aspergillum, into the pail and sprinkled holy water on the field. He made the sign of the cross in the air and was probably muttering something like this, "Heavenly Father, in Whom we live, and move, and have life, grant us rain in abundance, that, our temporal needs being met, we may seek with confidence your eternal gift." He prayed to God the Almighty for plenty of rain, enough rain to grow crops, enough rain to fill the well, and enough rain to keep Willow Creek flowing. "Through Christ, our Lord. Amen."

Because I spent a great deal of time climbing everything I could, and a few things I shouldn't, Mom started calling me her little monkey. The best climbing tree in our back yard was a sand plum tree that stood about thirty feet tall. It had a low crown where the trunk spread out into three main branches. When facing the tree, you could see it was an old woman inviting you to sit in her big lap. A large tree limb, her arm, growing to the right ran parallel to the ground. We used the low bough as a gymnastics horse. The center branch, her neck, the tallest branch of the tree rose straight up. I liked to climb the tall branch to enjoy a good view of our vegetable garden. To the left a medium sized branch, her other arm, rose at a forty-five-degree angle with a good perch at the end of the limb. That's where I liked to hang out most. That's where I decided to install my new tire swing.

I found some clothesline cord and used it instead of a proper rope. My dad and uncles were always improvising with things they already had on hand. Why shouldn't I? We didn't have an old car tire in Dad's garage or his rusty green and white metal shed but that didn't stop me either. I used an old bicycle tire instead. I tied the thin rope around the skinny bike tire and carried the rig up to my favorite spot. After tying the loose end of the cord to a solid branch I dropped the rope and tire which stopped several feet from the ground.

To try it out, I carefully lowered myself into the swing from above. As I descended, the rope twisted around my arm, maybe it snagged on my clothes, or maybe I simply lost my grip. Whatever happened, I fell – I fell hard – and the rope and flimsy tire twisted around my neck. After a few intense seconds of struggling I managed to untangle myself, threw the thing off, and fell to the ground.

I was dusting off my hand-me-down jeans when I heard someone coming out the back door. The screen door slammed shut and Mom walked onto the lawn still twinkling with morning dew. She could tell right away I was into some kind of mischief. Maybe she noticed my tousled hair, red face, or even my lack of breath. But I was always up in a tree looking like a hot mess and that's why she only said, "What are you doing out here, Stephen Mark?"

"Nothing Mom. I'm trying out my new tire swing."

Ask Mom, or Grandma Booms, I was always climbing trees, silos, or any other thing I could to get off the ground.

"What are you doing up there?" yelled Grandma Booms.

I had climbed to the top of a fifty-foot grain silo at the Booms's farm five miles west of Harbor Beach. Uncle Bob told me both silos were fifty feet tall, but the platform I was on was clearly higher than the other one. I liked going up there to sit with my thoughts on the small metal shelf attached to the silo for inspecting the chopped grain inside. I liked the sweet, slightly rotten smell rising from the silage, and didn't really care if I could fall in the fluffy stuff and die from suffocation. I liked sitting there, staring over the fields, looking toward Lake Huron. On a clear day you can see the deep blue streak of water, under the azure sky, where the land gives way to the freshwater sea.

Mom was always telling people I was her little monkey and she must've told Grandma Booms too. Maybe I was gone too long *or Grandma just knew where I was* and came looking for me. But there she was, the old woman, hands on her hips, looking up at me.

"Do you think you're a monkey? You're going to fall and break your neck. Come down from there right now."

"I like it up here, Grandma."

"You're going to get yourself killed."

"Bobby and I come up here all the time."

"That Uncle Robert of yours. He shouldn't be encouraging you. Are you hungry?"

"Yeah."

"Well okay then. Get down from there right now and come inside the house. I'll make you something to eat. Make sure you wash up first."

I climbed down from the silo while Grandma prayed that I wouldn't fall down and die.

"What's for lunch, Grandma?

"Chicken soup, bologna sandwiches, and there's some leftover hamburgers too."

Grandma and I sat down to pray. "Bless us, o Lord, and these, thy gifts which we are about to receive from the bounty of Christ, Our Lord. Amen."

Then we said the after-dinner prayer. "We thank thee, Almighty God, for all the benefits, who livest and reignest forever, world without end. Amen."

In Grandma's house we always said *both* prayers before eating because after supper the girls had to wash dishes and the boys had to do chores in the barn. There was no time for an after-dinner prayer after supper.

I liked eating Grandma Booms's food. She didn't cook German food, or any other kind of food, she simply cooked her way because she had an army to feed. Grandma introduced me to the hamburger sandwich. As a kid I hated eating a burger without the bun, but she didn't believe in buying buns when a couple slices of Lumber Jack Bread would be fine. But, especially for me, she cut two discs of bread, using a doughnut cutter, to make a tiny bun. She ate the crusts! I liked the bologna sandwiches she made too. She partially sliced each piece five times before cooking. This technique turns ordinary lunch meat into pink and black roses because the edges curled up in the frying pan.

All of us grandkids fought over her best mug, shaped like the Nestlé rabbit's head, when she made homemade milkshakes. Her other cups were boring plastic tumblers. She made incredible shakes with unpasteurized milk, chocolate powder, and vanilla ice cream from a two-gallon container she kept in the freezer downstairs. She used to make tons of chocolate chip cookies and kept most of them in the deep freeze and a couple dozen in a plastic box under her bed. "In case I get hungry in the middle of the night."

When you walked into her house she'd ask, "Did you eat?" before you had a chance to say hello. She wanted her thirty-five biological grandchildren, five adopted grandchildren, and several step-grandchildren to be well fed. She always offered her chicken lemon and rice soup. A huge pot of it was in the fridge at all times. Grandma Booms's soup wasn't fancy, but she knew her soup was good for you. In her simple chicken soup, she used instant rice, and lemon juice in a green glass bottle from the icebox. But the chicken, *the chicken,* you know she raised the chicken herself.

She incubated the eggs and raised the chicks in a little coop. Her farm had two coops, a small one to keep chicks in the spring and a bigger henhouse for egg-laying girls and the resident rooster. She collected the hens' eggs every day. When there were lots of bugs around for the yardbirds to eat she collected eggs twice a day. At harvest time, she dispatched the birds herself with a small hatchet. She placed their necks on a special log with two rusty nails on top to hold them in place. Afterward, the chickens ran around the back yard for several minutes with their heads cut off until they fell to the ground.

About ten years after Grandpa Booms passed away from cancer the farm was too much to handle and Grandma wanted to live in town. She moved to Bad Axe and built a new house which mimicked many features of her farmhouse in Harbor Beach. Her builder had to special order gray, diamond shaped shingles that resembled the roofing tiles on her old house. All of the siding, trim, and flashing had to be white, and the window shutters had to be painted her signature blue. She even had kitchen cupboards custom made out of the same inexpensive plywood used in her old kitchen. The same yellow paint on the kitchen walls. I bet she wanted to live out her days on the farm, but Uncle Bob wound up with it, *but goddamn,* you know she really missed the place.

No one was surprised how Grandma wrote her final testament. She took a copy of Grandpa's will, met with her attorney, crossed out her husband's name, wrote her name above his, and gave the document to the lawyer. Grandma out lived her husband by eighteen years. The old battle-axe!

Grandma Booms had arranged two final requests which nobody knew about. The family found a note pinned to her favorite dress, the one *she* wanted to wear, saying, *Take this to Ramsey's.* She also planned a surprise detour for her funeral procession by making arrangements with the Ramsey Funeral Home chauffer to drive her past the old farmstead in Harbor Beach *to see her home one last time.*

Dad started calling Wren *Tiny Bubbles* because he was drunk with patriarchal pride. I loved having her around because now I had a friend to play with. Wren and I liked to build an elaborate passenger train from dining room chairs and cushions from the couch. Dad was our number one passenger. He sat on a chair in the upper berth while Wren and I lay under the chairs in the lower berth.

My sister and I also liked camping in the back yard. Mom draped bed linens over the clothesline and staked the edges of the blankets to the ground with clothes pins. Then she'd put heavy blankets and a big pile of pillows on the ground for our bed.

A few years later after my other sister Contessa was born, all three of us liked playing church. We distributed Saltine crackers and pretended they were communion wafers, sipped Mom and Dad's homemade grape juice as a substitute for wine, and kneeled to pray. The juice stained our lips deep purple. When there was no grape juice in the fridge, we used grape Kool-Aid or tap water dyed with blue and red food coloring.

At our real church, Sacred Heart, the pipe organ could hold my interest during service, especially the loud parts of a solo or the drawn-out end of a song. I enjoyed singing hymns along with the congregation too. But I enjoyed looking at the art more. The wonderful polychromatic stained glass, the lifelike statues of Jesus, Mary, and Joseph, and the stone inlay of the Ave Maria symbol – a giant red calligraphic A on top of a blue M – its symmetry appealed to me. Another thing I liked about church was the ritual. The kneeling, the standing, the sitting. More kneeling, more standing, more sitting. It all felt right. I usually just pretended to pray. If I really prayed, I did it improperly by asking God for a cute girlfriend or a new portable cassette player with headphones. Who was going to hear my prayer anyway? Was it God? Did he have time to listen to me? I didn't know for sure.

Jezus, Maryja i Józef!

During service, I stared at the ceiling, my eyes following the arches and beams holding up the roof. Our church was no cathedral or mahogany beauty but it was well engineered and lovely in its simplicity. But the music, rituals, and building were not enough to keep me occupied. What I enjoyed best about attending church was watching the beautiful girls and women dressed in their Sunday best.

I checked out the ladies as they approached the alter for communion and ogled them again as they returned to their pews. Sure, I admired them with my eyes, but I enjoyed their perfume even more. Someone had given Mom a perfume sampler, a blue velvet lined box of miniatures, and I had smelled all of them. I even daubed the unctuous fragrances on my skin to try them out. *Mom never wore any of them.* She said they didn't smell like any flowers she knew of and they gave her a headache. The gals in church sprayed the perfume on heavy to compete with each other's narcotic fragrances and the priest's stonking incense burner.

A Catholic Mass ends after the priest gives his final blessing, then everyone sings praise, *because it's finally over,* as the priest, deacon, and altar boys exit the building. Some parishioners, anticipating a good breakfast and a good nap, would sneak out early. Other groups lingered. My family liked to linger, talking to other church members, chatting with Father Ansel Durham, and shooting the shit with people Mom and Dad knew from work.

One day, raring to go, I was out of the pew and down the aisle before anyone else. Before leaving the building, I dipped my hand into the silver, holy water cup and made a rapid sign of the cross. Outside, I waited on the sidewalk and goofed around next to Father Ansel's garage.

Father drove a big four door sedan. The driveway to his garage came up behind the church. Because each end had its own door, he could drive his big old boat all the way through the garage into the parking lot on the other side of the building. Next to his garage, they parked the church bus.

I went to the rusty school bus and tried getting inside by pulling on the front door. It wouldn't budge. I tried the fire escape in back but it wouldn't move either. I really wanted to go inside and play but I couldn't get in.

I started kicking pebbles and stones in the parking lot. Bored with that I kicked at clods of dirt in the carefully groomed beds. They were gorgeous. I was leaning down taking a deep whiff of the colorful flowers when Mom and Dad came out with some people I didn't know. They saw me goofing around in the flowerbeds.

Mom said, "Be careful with Father Ansel's roses."

"Yes, Steve, Father works so hard on them."

"*I am being careful.*"

"He's a bit sensitive."

"And, he's shy."

The strange man said, "But he is a *smart one,* isn't he?"

"You bet I'm smart. Mom even says so."

"He's already reading, Dr. Woods."

"Really? That's interesting, Charlie."

With a broad smile, Dad said, "Yes, sir."

"Good, good. Doesn't seem shy to me. He's doing pretty good from what I can see."

"What do you mean, doc?"

"Well, you know Buckley, you better keep an eye on that boy of yours. *Keep a close eye on him.* He's a real womanizer."

Driving home from church I climbed in front leaving Wren in back, strapped to my old duck taped car seat.

"Did you hear what Dr. Woods said, Steve? He says you're a real lady's man. You're all set then, huh?"

When we got home, Mom made French toast because I didn't want pancakes. While she whisked the eggs, cinnamon, and vanilla, Dad rummaged around in the fridge and took out a large ring of Polish sausage to fry for our big afternoon brunch. He clutched the sausage in his hands, held it in front of his crotch, and poked it into Mom's butt.

"Buckley Kubacki!"

"Oolala!"

Mom finished a huge stack of French toast and brought it to the table. She poured milk and homemade grape juice for everyone. I piled my plate with breakfast foods, spread a big glob of margarine on the French toast, and poured a puddle of fake maple syrup on the toast and sausage. I ate methodically, cutting bits of sausage, then a bit of toast, going back and forth, swirling each bite in the pool of oily syrup, washing it all down with gulps of grape juice, and big slugs of skim milk.

My little sister Tessa was born on a mild winter day. I remember it distinctly because Wren and I had caught chicken pox from one of our cousins at the start of Advent. Tessa's birthday was early enough in December that it wouldn't *ruin* Christmas. As a baby, Tessa stunned us with her beautiful light blonde hair. Wren and I started out as dirty blondes, and Jacob, born later, started out blonde too. But Contessa kept her blonde hair for life.

Grandpa Kubacki had passed many family traditions to Dad and our old man shared some of them with us that year. On Christmas Eve, he showed us how to leave a box of straw out for Baby Jesus, imitating the manger he slept in at Bethlehem. He told us Baby Jesus would come to our house during the night and sleep peacefully in our improvised cradle. The next morning, we knew He had been there because of the imprint in the hay. We all looked at the make-shift crib with amazement, and for myself a bit of disbelief, before tearing open our gifts. I figured the settling hay was from gravity.

Dad showed us another cool thing on New Year's Eve. He cut an apple in half as a foretelling of the year just like *Dziadzo* did. I noticed how carefully Dad selected the apple. A big, round, juicy one. He gently removed the stem, laid the apple on its side, carefully sliced it in half on the horizontal, separated the halves, unfolded it like a child's picture book, and showed us two perfect five-point stars made by the pattern of apple seeds.

Dad smiled and said, "It's going to be a good year. You see here? The two stars are perfect. Both of them have five points and the two halves mirror each other."

I knew the fullness and symmetry of the fruit was the real secret. But with three little Kubacki cherubs in his house it would be a good year, it would be a very good year.

Having baby Tessa in the house sparked memories of Wren and me. As all moms do, ours liked to reminisce and share embarrassing stories about us. She told me I had a great potty-training, and if you ever met her, she would tell you the same thing. Mom would definitely tell you about the time I put a marble in my butt. I stuck the thing up there to see how it felt, couldn't get it out, and had to ask Mom for help. After all, she is a nurse.

When she told this story, she would tell you how her and Dad almost had to intervene with an enema. In our house, if chamomile tea didn't fix your digestive tract problems a douche from the hot water bottle would take care of you.

But I didn't let them near me with that red rubber bottle. I said, "I'll poop it out."

Mom sat on the edge of the bathtub watching, waiting, coaching me until I pushed it out. When the marble fell in the water it made a gentle plop and a quiet tink as it hit the bottom of the bowl.

As a youngster, I had learned good bathroom habits and everything was going well. I used the miniature toilet with no problem and graduated to the big boy toilet in no time. As I flushed down a turb, I was told to say, "Goodbye poo-poo," to avoid some weird Freudian separation anxiety. No problem, no problems at all, except I pissed the bed at night, often, much too often.

Mom got frustrated dealing with the urine-soaked laundry and especially irritated with the soiled mattress she had to scrub. Once I had wet the bed five or six times she had had enough. After stripping the soiled linens and blankets, cleaning the mattress and allowing it to dry out in the sun, she installed an industrial grade enuresis mattress pad with thick plastic backing. Happy with the preventative measures she said, "Heck, that should do the trick."

Lemon

A ditch which runs straight into the headwater of the Pinnebog River surrounds the small woods behind my childhood home. The ditch, once a pleasant brook, was dug deeper and wider to drain the Huron County Fairgrounds, the south swamp, and several farms at the edge of town. It was named for one of the farmers, William Bissett. Every summer we used to find tadpoles, frogs, and turtles in the ditch. In the winter the water was so crisp and clean we figured it was good enough to drink. It's called the Bisset Drain, now spelled with a *single t.* We just called it the ditch.

Along the ditch is a grassy field and an old apple orchard. Behind the little woods is the county fairgrounds. When they dredged the Bisset Drain, the dug-up gravel, sand, and muck was left behind creating spoil banks and a good-sized spoil tip. Our trail laid on top of the long spoil bank through the woods and the spoil tip was our sledding hill. The perfect sledding spot for a bunch of bored, small-town kids.

Dad bought a steel rail sled for my siblings and me. He bought it when we we're quite young – Tessa was still a baby – there wasn't a single chip in the shiny red paint and the rope was crisp without any frayed ends. I used the sled for pulling my sisters around the yard, back and forth on the sidewalk, and Mom enjoyed dragging us around the yard too.

One year before I could use the sled, Dad said it needed some maintenance to keep it in good shape. He sealed the steering board and plywood deck with linseed oil, brushing it on thick. After the oil soaked in, we used an old dish rag to polish it. He showed me how to grease the steering rail pivots with dabs of Vaseline and we borrowed some paraffin wax from Mom's canning jar cupboard to lubricate the steel runners.

The sled was ready.

Me, and two kids my age, Coby Dreher and Stosh Zajac, took the sled back in the woods after an ice storm. Zajac has a familiar name but he's not my cousin. We tried to figure out *if we were cousins.* We decided he was cousin to my cousins, but not a cousin to me. This seems to happen a lot in Huron County.

The air was heavy. Frost was forming around my mouth and inside my nostrils. The brush bent under the weight of heavy snow. It reflected gleaming light everywhere, like a mirrored ball you'd see in a movie with too much disco dancing. The hill was already slick from other kids in the neighborhood sledding, but when we tried the steel rail sled the runners cut into the packed snow and it flew down the slope to the ditch below. Dreher, Zee, and I made runs to the bottom, climbed back to the top of the spoil tip, and did it again, and again.

Coby had brought his eight-foot-long toboggan along, a huge wooden deck lashed with rope handles along the sides. The front of the sled coiled up in a cee like a giant candy cane. Loaded-up with the three of us it floated down the hill. We figured out how to stand on the sled, using the rope to stabilize us, and rode it like a snowboard. Usually, we made it down in one piece but no one was standing when the thing slammed into the bottom of the ditch.

After one of our crashes this gangly kid appeared at

the edge of the snow-covered field near the ditch.

He said, “Hey kid, let me try that toboggan.”

Two other big kids from the block came to the edge of the ditch. They insisted on using our other sleds too.

One of the other ones said, “Yeah, give me that sled.”

We watched as they took my sled, Coby’s toboggan, and Stosh’s saucer.

I had never seen a flying saucer sled before Stosh got his for Christmas. It’s a sled made for one rider. A shallow plastic dish with a handle on each side. While riding it, you could sail straight down the hill or with a slight twist before launching, spin down the hill, spinning, spinning, spinning, all the way down.

We knew the tall, gangly kid. He had shown us some grown-up stuff in the ditch a couple of times before. One day, he had caught us writing our names in the snow with piss. He talked us into dropping our pants and sucking each other’s dicks. After that day, he kept coming around to tamper with us.

These guys were older, much bigger boys, and the fucking dopes couldn’t figure out how to work my metal rail sled. They threw it aside after a couple of runs. It landed upside down at the edge of the ditch. They kept trying to stand on the toboggan without falling down and kept trying to spin the saucer without falling out. But they were too big and clumsy and couldn’t manage either one.

Trying again, two of the clods came barreling down the hill on the big toboggan. They made it all the way down while standing but careened off the ditch bank and slammed into my upended sled. The last punk, on Stosh's sled, made a run down the hill. He was skinny enough to get it spinning all the way to the bottom of the hill where he hit the toboggan, ran over his buddies, crashed into the metal rails of my sled, broke the saucer, spilled out of the broken dish, and rolled to the ground.

The hoodlums got up and pulled themselves together.

The gangly, funny looking kid, Bentley Snock, was angry. He chewed on his bloody lip, sneered at us, and said, "See ya later, suckers." He kicked Zee's broken saucer, scattering it into bits of light blue shrapnel.

Everybody in our elementary school saw the movie, a boring documentary in the gymnasium. The principle, all the teachers, even the janitor saw it, and you've seen ones like it too. We've all seen films about the evils of cigarette smoking. A former smoker explains his bad habit, why he's deformed, and why he can't speak properly because of a tube sticking out of his throat. Wearing the obligatory white lab coat, a surgeon cuts open the healthy pink lungs of a non-smoker and then cuts open the blackened lungs of a smoker. *Oh man, that is so fucking cool.* It was irresistible. We had to try smoking.

After school, Coby, Stosh, and I went straight home and rolled our own cigarettes. We did the best we could without tobacco or Zig-Zags. Used lined composition paper. Sealed the empty tubes with spit, like a cowboy. Cigarettes might not kill you, but those evil paper tubes we rolled almost did. They were harsh as hell with absolutely no flavor. Nothing but a mighty strong paper hit.

Those kinds of educational films warned us about nuclear war, how your teeth would rot from poor dental care, and how to prevent forest fires. We laughed at nuclear Armageddon, the dangers of smoking, and tooth decay.

Fire didn't scare my friends and me. At least not your everyday fires. We knew how to build campfires and stoke a pot-bellied stove. But the big fires, devastating fires that burned your house to the ground, or a harrowing forest fire, they scared the shit out of us.

One day after school, Coby, Stosh, and I were walking down Dreher's driveway to the back of Coby's house. About to enter the mudroom, we saw smoke billowing over the cedar hedge. The smoke was coming from beyond Mr. Dreher's well-tended vegetable garden. The small field behind Dreher's place was charred black, red embers sizzled on top of white patches of ash, and soot fluttered in the air.

If we didn't do something, all of South Street would burn down and the fire would spread through the whole town. If the wind blew the right way it would spread across the whole thumb area, like the Great Thumb Fire of 1881. This blaze behind my house could reach Harbor Beach and Grandpa Booms's barn would catch fire like it did when Mom was a little girl back on the farm in the 1950s.

Mom said Grandpa had to use his biggest ladder from his barn. The long rickety one for climbing up to the hayloft. Grandpa found the damn thing sitting at the edge of the holding lot, a misplaced pitchfork and crow bar were also fortuitously nearby. Grandpa propped the big ladder against the flaming barn and climbed to the top. He tore off some of the siding and scooped out a huge fireball from the tinder box inside. Men from neighboring farms showed up and helped empty the hay loft using torn-off planks of siding as shovels. The men swept the smoldering straw into the wet cow manure in the lot below. It took nearly all night, but Grandpa and the other farmers put out the fire and saved his barn. The following day my uncles fertilized the fields with the burnt straw, ashes, and cow shit.

Most of Braeburn's orchard was cloaked in smoke. We couldn't do anything about the field next to Coby's house, it was already burned. Mr. Foster's walking trail had turned to coal, but there was still a green line along the edge of the ditch.

We ran through the smoke directly towards the fire and pulled our shirts over our noses making effective filters like we had learned about in the film at school. We peeled off our jackets and swatted the ground because we didn't have a chemical fire extinguisher or a military grade blanket.

We were covered in black and completely exhausted. My new tennis shoes were trashed and so was everything else I was wearing. Coby and Stosh looked the same, covered in soot, their clothes ruined. But we all stood smiling and laughing in the spent field because we had saved Huron County from another Great Fire.

We sat on the edge of the ditch trying to catch our

breath. I was thinking about an ice-cold Coca-Cola, maybe a Popsicle, and some potato chips. Mrs. Dreher's kitchen was waiting for us. She always had the best snacks.

Getting up and heading back to Coby's house we saw our neighbor, Mike Braeburn, walking towards us with a pitchfork in his hand. He was smiling, but he was always smiling.

"Well, hello boys. You're a mess. What happened?"

We told him about the forest fire film at school and our heroic efforts battling the dangerous fire in his field.

Mike said, "Indubitably," while looking at us with glimmering eyes. He told us we had done the right thing by fighting the fire. Reaching down, he picked up a piece of burnt sod, smiled, and told us how fire clears the weeds allowing wildflowers to grow. How large forest fires clear underbrush allowing the big trees to grow. And that Mother Nature doesn't always provide and sometimes we need to help her out.

He crumbled the sod and dropped it to the earth.

"I lit this fire, boys."

We had saved Huron County from Mike's ferocious controlled burn.

Two

My buddies and I flew kites like a lot of kids do. To do it, you unwind thirty feet of string, lay it on the ground with the kite tied to one end, and then run as fast as you can. When that fails, you do it again, and again, until you catch the wind and the kite goes aloft. On a windy day, you can simply let the kite go as it rises straight up and rips into the air. Almost all kites need a tail to stabilize it, but we each had one of these new things that didn't need a tail. It looked like an enormous bat with large, evil looking, yellow and orange eyes.

The black bat kite was nearly impossible to crash. Even in a bad crosswind it could stay in the air. It dived to the ground, a few inches from impact, pulled into an upward spiral, corrected itself, and rose high into the air again. The thing hardly ever crashed. It was crazy.

We wanted to send one of our kites a mile high. A bat kite comes with a small spool of string and the package said it was two hundred feet. With three kites we had six hundred feet of line to put one kite high up in the sky. Six hundred feet was not going to be enough. Not even close to a mile.

I said, "We need more string. Maybe twenty-five or twenty-six spools to get it a mile high."

Coby said, "We don't have any more."

"One of us has to go to the store. Who wants to go?" Zee asked.

Coby and I shrugged our shoulders.

"Okay, I'll go."

We pulled money out of our pockets and handed it

to Zee. He grabbed his bike, rode down the trail and up the street to the end of the block. He was back from Five and Dime in twenty minutes.

Still breathing hard from his ride, he said, "I got twelve more rolls. That's all I could get."

"That's over half a mile. Close enough."

Coby said, "Whatever, it will still be cool."

One after another, we tied them onto the kite line and let the spools into the air. The line developed an amazing amount of drag. It looked like it was a mile high, but it was only three thousand feet. It was way down at the end of South Street. We could see the small triangular black speck which seemed to be above the water tower next to the library.

We had watched the *mile high kite* for only a few minutes when, with a crisp zing, the string snapped. The tiny black triangle spiraled down from the sky and crashed into a tall silver maple tree in front of the county jail. Our bat kite sat in the giant tree for a long-ass time. It was in the tree for years, falling to pieces bit by bit, until the last chunk of black plastic blew away in the wind.

Someone planted several apple trees behind the houses on my block. Probably, Mike Braeburn. About twenty trees scattered in the field behind my house all the way down to Coby's back yard. I bet it used to be an orchard filled with trees but most of them were already cut down when I was a kid.

In late spring, too impatient for the fruit to ripen,

we ate green apples off the trees. We took a couple of bites, spat it out, threw away the sour apple, and picked another one to nibble on. For some reason, we always got upset stomachs.

I knew the Drehers since I was young boy. They had a good house on a good lot with a big arborvitae hedge growing near their garage. The hedge drew a line between a small yard behind their house and the garden at the rear of the property. They grew a lot of the same things we did, salad fixings, carrots, green beans, potatoes, tomatoes, and spindly stalks of sweet corn. A giant cherry tree lived at the edge of the garden and competed with the veggies for water. Beyond the garden was the old apple orchard.

Mr. Dreher's a good guy, but you should've seen him when Coby and I pulled up some onions from his garden. Coby's old man had specially prepared a sandy patch in the garden for raising carrots and onions. Man was he pissed.

We had pulled up a row of his carefully tended, big, juicy, sweet onions, and used them as projectiles. We trashed the patch, ruined our clothes, and smashed his onions all over the yard. After the onion fight, we heard the mudroom door slam and hid behind the neighbor's shed. We sat tittering trying not to giggle. I'm pretty sure Mr. Dreher could smell us. When he found us, he whipped our asses with his bare hands. That was the only time I received corporal punishment as a kid. My parents often threatened to spank me, but they never did. I'd laugh at them when they tried to swat me.

Mr. Dreher built a tree fort for us under the limbs

of three of his apple trees. He dug holes and installed four sturdy posts. Three feet from the ground he built a platform with a small hole in the center of the deck. Built four walls of plywood running halfway up the structure and made the top half of the shack walls from corrugated steel sheeting.

I don't remember if the fort had a roof. If it did, it only covered part of it because you could see the sky through the tree branches. Playing inside you could smell sweet white apple blossoms in the spring and the putrid funk of rotten apples in the fall.

Coby, Wren, and I were fooling around, playing doctor in the fort one afternoon. She didn't come in there often because we had an official policy of *No Girls Allowed*. But she didn't count as a girl to us. My sister enjoyed dirt, mud, and bugs as much as any boy, but wouldn't bait a worm on her fishing hook because they wiggled too much. The three of us were in the fort when the kid from down the block, that funny looking kid, Bentley Snock, popped up through the floor and climbed into the fort.

Snock lived in a rundown camper trailer on the outskirts of town. It sat in a field overgrown with tall grass and stubborn weeds. The junkyard owned Snock's dilapidated trailer and the land surrounding it. His family – two adults and four kids, just like mine – shared a tiny galley kitchen and a cramped bathroom. The kids slept in two narrow bunk beds at one end of the trailer, while Bentley's parents slept on the kitchen table which converted into bed using the bench cushions as a mattress.

Snock stood there, looking at us with a lupine grin.

He was there to tamper with us like he had in the ditch and the woods. He had shown things to us, and dared us to be men, even though he was only about ten or eleven years old himself. *Some man he was.*

All the boys on the block seemed to hang out with Snock *or at least he was always hanging out with them.* He was a juvenile sexual delinquent, big words I didn't know back then, and he could always find prey because there were lots of boys four, five, or six years younger than him running loose, isolated from care and protection, in our laissez-faire neighborhood.

Wren was a tomboy and liked hanging out with Coby and me, but she happened to be there that day, in the wrong place, at the wrong time.

Snock removed something from his pocket. There was a bright snap, and a quick flash of silver as he unfolded the small knife. He held the sharp blade against my neck and told Wren, "Take off your panties." With a look of terror on her face she did as she was told. He pressed the pointed steel blade against my jugular and said, "I'll fucking kill your brother if you tell anybody about this."

I don't think Bentley knew what to do *with her.* He might have been thinking, *Is she going to act different than boys on the block? What should I do to her? What will this girl do afterward? Would she tell someone? Or shut the fuck up like the boys in the neighborhood?*

Snock's face was expressionless as he stared at her.

Wren put her clothes back on.

He grinned at us and slithered away like a snake.

We were too naïve to understand and too young to stop him.

After he left, I lowered myself through the hole in the floor and my shirt caught on the plywood. The rough-cut board lifted the shirt and exposed my abdomen. Struggling, I unsnagged myself, lost my grip, went through the hole, and badly scraped my belly as I fell to the ground.

I screamed.

Coby and I were seven, and Wren was five years old, we told no one about it, and soon enough, I forgot about his threat to kill me.

When Wren and I got home, Mom was upset and asked us, "What did you do?"

She and my sister cleaned me up with soap, water, and bubbly peroxide.

"He fell through the door in Coby's fort."

"You've ruined your shirt. Look what you've done. Oh, heck."

Mom finished cleaning the abrasions while I stood in front of the bathroom sink. She applied some Porter's salve and placed a large gauze pad on the abrasion. The heady scent of camphor and cloves wafted up as she wrapped my abdomen with an elastic bandage. She took me to my bedroom and I sat down on the bed. She kissed me on the forehead, left my room, and went to the other end of the house.

You returned to the bathroom and stood on a footstool at the sink. You looked into the medicine cabinet mirror expecting a frown, a smile, something, anything. But there was absolutely nothing on your face.

You walked back to the room, lay down on the bed, and rolled onto your side. Bringing your knees to your chest, you faced the lavender wall and stared at an empty sphere. The void in front of your face. It's a spot in front of everyone's face. A place where you can put yourself, and when you're there, in that place, you can look from there back at yourself here.

Before a wood furnace could be installed in our house someone from the city had to inspect the chimney. The inspector issued a permit even though things weren't quite ready. He said we needed to hire a professional chimney sweep, but Dad decided we could do the job ourselves.

We got forty feet of thick rope, a ball of chicken wire, a heavy pipe wrench, and climbed our wobbly aluminum ladder to the rooftop. Dad told me the plan.

He tied the rope to the handle of the pipe wrench and dropped it down the red brick smokestack. After five or ten feet fell into the shaft he stopped the rope. We attached the chicken wire to the rope and laid the end of the rope on the rooftop. Dad went to the basement.

I lowered the rope while Dad waited in the basement for the wrench to appear at the chimney inspection door. He untied the knot and removed the wrench. He came back to the roof and sent me to the basement.

I knelt at the bottom of the chimney looking up through the inspection door. Up on the roof, Dad made the first upward pull. When my rope got to the end, I tugged it, giving Dad the signal to stop pulling. Then I pulled the rope down. We had a tug-of-war through the shaft and cleaned the shit out of that chimney with that ball of chicken wire. Afterward, Dad's gloves and coat were dirty with soot and I was completely covered in black.

Our new wood burning furnace was almost as big as the old fuel oil furnace. How could this behemoth be more efficient? Wood fired ovens and pot-bellied stoves aren't this big. Nina and Rusty heated their whole house with a wood stove in the basement. The heat radiated up through floor vents and they used a box fan to move the warm air around upstairs. *Now that's efficient.*

Dad told me our new furnace could burn eight-foot-long pieces of wood, but most people only burned two- or three-foot-long sticks in them. That's what we did. Sometimes we kicked on the oil burner to light a fire, but usually lit fires with scrap paper, cardboard, and matches.

We could have installed an automatic vent to admit air to the fire through the ash pit door, but instead, we left the door ajar to let air into the fire. Never did install the cable operated vent. Mom just yelled at one of us kids after the fire was roaring, "Go close the ash pit door!" She usually hollered at me.

Mom had to show me how to build a fire, "In case your father or I can't take care of it." But I already knew how to do it. You start small and build up the fire. Add pieces of paper, twigs, and bits of dry bark. You pile on bigger, and bigger pieces of wood until you get a good blaze going.

We had to clean out the ash pit when it got too full. Using a garden trowel, Dad and I scooped and scraped ashes from the pit into metal pails. I carried the buckets to the garden trying not to make a mess going up the stairs. It was a pain in the ass.

Dad and I finally built an ash bin one fine winter day. He showed me how to use tin snips. We cut and folded the sheet metal into a long rectangular box. It fit perfectly in the ash pit.

Dad got the fuel oil tank topped off – it lasted a couple years. He cut a little bit of wood, bought some firewood too, and to supplement it, bought crate and pallet scraps. A man from a factory in town pulled up in a small dump truck and dumped a load of wood on our driveway. We removed the basement window – it was so easy to remove – and threw the wood into the furnace room.

Most of the wood was crappy softwood, it burned hot and fast. The wood had a funky odor and stunk up the whole basement until it dried. There was a bit of good hardwood, some oak and maple, but not much. The factory used most of the hardwood to make pallet stringers.

It was a good thing we got the super-efficient furnace because money was tight when Dad got laid off from the slaughterhouse, started working at another one, and then left that slaughterhouse. He was sick of it and started working in the meat department at a grocery store in town and became friends with another butcher, Stan Garner. His family was into gardening like ours, *but the Garners were seriously into it.* They had a regular veggie garden, sure, but they also ran a tomato farm with acres of fragrant tomato plants. They grew Roma, Beefsteak and Early Girl tomatoes.

Both of our families canned or froze almost everything we grew in our gardens. Stan got us into making fresh pressed apple juice because he knew a man, over in Elkton, with a cider press. Bucka and Stan asked owners of abandoned apple orchards if we could pick their fruit. Sometimes, we went on the property of overgrown orchards, without asking permission, and helped ourselves. My old man often ventured into places he didn't belong.

Years later, while my parents were on vacation in Arizona, Dad picked some wild lemons and oranges from the hotel grounds where they were staying. When they returned from the trip, Dad asked Mom to make lemon meringue pie from his pilfered produce. Mom said she had to double, maybe triple, the amount of sugar called for in the recipe to make the bitter fruit somewhat edible. The pie tasted like hell, it was awful, it was so awful Dad could only eat *half a pie.*

It's unbelievable, but those ugly, wormy, scaly apples made delicious cider. All the different varieties we collected and blended together produced incredible, crisp juice. We drank a lot of it fresh from the press, stored some in green pickle pails – those great sliced pickles from McDonald's – pressure canned some of it, and Dad and Mr. Garner always let a few gallons go hard to make homemade apple wine. They called it apple jack.

Dad was open to nearly any venture Stan suggested, so naturally our families raised and slaughtered chickens together. We kept the birds at Garner's place because they had plenty of room on their farm. Stan and his youngest son, Billy, built a small henhouse next to an abandoned spearmint field which refused to stop growing, they tried, they really tried, but they just couldn't kill the crap. Dad and Stan dispatched the birds, Billy and I plucked the feathers with a giant spinning wire brush, Mrs. Garner gutted, and Mom cut them into little pieces.

When Dad told Mr. Garner about our new furnace and the benefits of wood heat, the Garners installed a Franklin Stove to heat their house by the end of that summer. Because of the need for fuel, and the do-it-yourself nature of our families, we started cutting firewood together.

Behind my house on a sunny summer day, I was lying in the tall grass staring at the sky. There wasn't a single bird in the air, not a hawk, sparrow, or robin in the pale blue heavens. Only random shapes of fluffy clouds, spilled out of God's jigsaw puzzle box, assembled into shapes inside my head. The field was filled with wildflowers. Everything was in bloom. Pink and blue bachelor buttons, yellow daisies with their sad, dark eyes, and dainty white flowers had popped up everywhere. The clouds were floating by as the afternoon rolled on, when I heard bike chains rattling and laughter near the street. The noise was coming toward me.

I sat up.

Two boys were riding their bikes up the trail from the street. One kid wore a baseball cap over his shaggy hair. The other one only wore a grin.

Derrick saw me sitting in the weeds and said,

"What are you doing, Kubacki?"

Boyd said, "Hey Kubacki."

"Hey Hogan, hey Boyd. What are you guys doing?"

"We're looking for the trail to the fairgrounds."

"We heard you can get in for free."

"Well, maybe. But this is private property."

"Is this land yours?"

"No. It belongs to Mike Braeburn."

"He won't mind if we use it, will he?"

"Nah, he won't mind."

"You know he would, and so do I."

"What do you mean?"

"I mean you can't use the trail."

Derrick said, "Come on Kubacki, do you know where the trail is or not?"

"Of course, I know where it is. It's my back yard. But I already said you can't ride the trail. You guys got to leave."

"But my brother told me there's a trail here. He said it's right across from the dirt baseball field on South Street. It's got to be here somewhere."

"Yeah, Kubacki, he said we could take the trail straight through the woods to the fairgrounds."

"You guys can't use it."

"Yes, we will. It's right there. I can see it."

"Fuck yeah we will."

Hogan and Boyd took off on their bikes and peddled to the top of the sledding hill before I could pull my bike out of the weeds. I jumped onto my bike and chased them into the woods. When I reached the top of the hill, they had already gone past the big aspen tree leaning over the trail into the ditch – they managed to duck under it just in time. The trail follows the excavated spoils of the drain and forms a meandering path on top of the small mounds of dirt. The bumpy trail bounces you left and right, and up and down, the entire way. Boyd veered off toward the ditch. He didn't crash in the dry ditch bed but came to a stop in the brush. Derrick passed Boyd on the right and rode ahead of him. Boyd made it out of the brush, got back on his bike, and continued down the winding path. I was behind Derrick now and Boyd was behind me. I pulled up to Derrick, grinded my front wheel into his rear wheel, and smashed my axle into his spokes.

"He's ramming me, Boyd."

"Peddle faster!"

Hogan stopped, I crashed into him, and Boyd crashed into me. I threw my bike to the ground and yelled, "You guys can't use my fucking trail!"

But it was no use. Derrick and Boyd took off on their bikes again. I caught up to Boyd at a wide spot where the trail branches off into the woods. I rammed my front wheel into his rear wheel as he crested the hill at the end of the trail.

Boyd hollered, "Kubacki's going crazy!"

He fell into the brush as I passed him.

Derrick rolled down the hill, crashed into the single plank foot bridge, and fell into the ditch.

I came down the hill, crossed the plank, rode up the hill on the other side of the ditch, and pedaled to the edge of the dusty horse track. I stood by the track waiting, bike parked behind me, hands on my hips.

"This is my woods and it's my trail. I told you guys

you can't use it."

They got up out of the ditch, brushed themselves off, and walked to the edge of the racetrack.

"Hey Kubacki," Hogan said, "that was cool."

"Yeah, I thought you were going crazy."

"Oh, yeah? Nah, I was just goofing around with you guys."

"I got to get home. It's almost six."

"Yeah, me too, got to be home before the whistle."

"All right, guys. I'll see you tomorrow."

"See ya later, Kubacki!"

"Yeah, see ya, Kubacki. Later."

I got on my bike and rode through the woods back to my house.

I started hanging out at Hogan's house. It was cool having a friend that didn't live on my street. Almost everyone I knew lived on my block. At first, Mom didn't want me riding to the south side of town, but eventually I convinced her it was okay.

"My buddies and I are always playing in the woods, riding the trails, or hanging out at the fairgrounds. The barns are over there, where Mr. Braeburn keeps his horse, Little Mike. Coby, Stosh, and I go to the stables all the time. Derrick's house is right by the barns."

Two cute girls from school, the Glen sisters, lived next door to Hogan. One day at Derrick's house, he suggested stealing bras and panties from the neighbor's clothesline. Boyd and I thought it would be fun and agreed to do it.

The lady next door finished hanging out her wash and went inside the house. We waited until the coast was clear, ran across Derrick's yard into the neighbor's yard, grabbed a few articles of wet clothing from the line, and ran back into Hogan's house with our plunder.

We looked at the underwear. I wasn't thinking about the girls who wore the clothes but was wondering how they put these things on. *Especially the bras.* How the hell do they work? With the twisty elastic band and complicated clips how could a girl connect the two ends of the string behind her back? And wow! The panties! They're so damn sheer and flimsy. It's only a thin piece of fabric and some frilly lace.

The woman next door had seen us and probably didn't want to deal with three stupid boys, so the next day she came over and talked to Mrs. Hogan. The two ladies spoke on the front porch for a few minutes. Derrick's mom said goodbye and stomped inside to have a talk with us.

Mrs. Hogan came into the living room.

"I just spoke with Mrs. Glen. She said you and your friends made a panty raid and stole her daughters' unmentionables from their clothesline yesterday. Did you boys steal those girls' laundry?"

Derrick answered, "Yeah, um, no."

"Goddamn it, Derrick, I've got enough headaches! You boys stay out of the neighbor's yard."

He reached for the remote control, turned up the volume, and nodded his head as we watched *The Three Stooges.*

Lemon

My brother Jacob was born the week I entered second grade. I love my two sisters, but I'd had it with them. I wanted a little brother. I needed someone to rough house with.

When Jake was a couple of years old, we did stunts with my BMX bike and our little red wagon. I rode the bike with Jake in the wagon – a thin chain dangling between us – pulling him over a ramp to send him flying into the air or fishtailing the wagon until he crashed. I'd do anything to make him crash. After each crash, I tied him into the bed of wagon, ensuring his safety, and we made another run.

Wren helped me pad him up with a hundred layers of pants, sweatshirts, and jackets, and even though kids never wore helmets in the 70s, she made Jake wear Dad's metallic blue motorcycle helmet. The oversized dome bobbled on his tiny head. When he crashed, he bounced up from the wreck, giggled like a girl, and shouted, "Let's do it again, Steve."

"All right, Jake. Let's go!"

Wren and Contessa had wanted another sister to play dress-up, school, and house. They got their wish anyway when Jake was born because he would let my sisters paint his face with their makeup and dress him in their clothes. One time the girls dressed Jacob in Wren's Girl Scout uniform and Mom snapped a picture of *my three sisters.* It's in the family album. The girls liked playing school so much with my kid brother that both of them became teachers.

Jake enjoyed throwing the ball around and cracking a few with the bat in the yard. Dad was usually too busy to practice with him and I didn't like to play sports. I was a bookworm, not a jock. He practiced his pitch by throwing a tennis ball at the wall of Dad's tool shed. He threw the ball over and over and wore a hole in the old reclaimed barn siding. Jacob tried out for Little League and made the team. My brother played baseball until the end of high school. He was good. He was good enough to try out for the Wolverines when he studied engineering at University of Michigan.

Is there a sports gene? If there is, I don't have a strand of it. I failed to place on a team for Little League tryouts. During gym class, I was usually picked last for any team sport. Being uncoordinated, maybe because I had to wear leg braces as a young boy, I couldn't play sports well. I wanted to play sports, but was too clumsy and hadn't learned the basic skills.

One day at the ballpark, I was batboy while my buddies played a scrimmage. A kid was swinging his bat, warming up for the pitch, when I got too close. I misinterpreted his motions and thought he was done swinging. The batter took another swing as I picked up a stray bat near home plate. His bat came rushing at me as he followed through.

I took a wild hit to the belly and was damn lucky my inguinal hernia didn't rupture on the spot. Clutching at my gut in agony, gasping and trying to catch my breath, I stumbled to my bike. Couldn't possibly ride it, I just leaned against it like an old man with a walker, trudged across the street, and went home.

Dad liked to catch up with paperwork on Sunday mornings after church when his boss, Mr. Paigne, wasn't around looking over his shoulder. The rest of the family came along because we enjoyed shopping in Paigne's Five and Dime with absolutely no customers around. Mom, Wren, and Contessa looked for clothes, with Jake crawling around on the deep shag carpet trying to stay out of their way. While they tried on outfits and Dad worked in the office, I went to the basement to play in the sporting goods and toy departments.

The old building originally housed two stores, each with their own basement. The two foundations had different floor levels but they were connected by gentle ramps throughout the warehouse. The storeroom floor rose and fell in smooth ascending and descending ramps to compensate for the uneven floors. Me and the owner's son, Mitch, liked to ride skateboards and bikes from store stock during business hours, but it was definitely more fun riding up and down the ramps when I had the whole basement to myself. The warehouse was an underground skate park and with all the merchandise shelves to maneuver around it was like being inside a maze.

Upstairs, there was a hunting and pocketknife display case. I had noticed where the clerk hid the key and could open the case anytime to look at the knives. One day, I removed a jackknife, carefully opened the box, unrolled the wax paper, and unfolded the brand-new blade. It made a satisfying click as it opened, had a locking blade, a dark wood handle, and shiny brass rivets. After looking at it, I folded it, put it back in the box, placed it in the display case, and locked the door.

Quite often, I went to the Brach's Pick-A-Mix and roasted nut counter and snacked on nuts and candy. Almost everybody that worked there enjoyed a handful of candy or nuts now and then. Mitch, Mr. Paigne, Mrs. Paigne, and even my old man did it. The best was finding a nigger toe – a Brazil nut – in the mixed nuts. Everyone said not to call them that, because they knew better, but that's what a lot of people, including me, called them anyway.

I ate a Neapolitan candy, chewed it up fast, and swallowed it. Then I had a chocolate caramel. Let it melt in my mouth for a few seconds and gobbled it down. I ate a handful of cashews. Some salty flavor to contrast with the sweets. Through the greasy glare of the nut bar glass, I looked toward the knife case and smiled. I walked to the checkout, reached for the cashier's hidden key, opened the display, and took out a brand-new hunting knife with its own leather sheath. It had a curved blade like a scimitar. It looked dangerous. I put it in my pocket and took it home. *Nobody would miss it, would they?*

Soon, I had a good knife collection. Small knives, big knives, lock blade knives, and the curved blade hunting knife, the first one I had stolen. No one ever asked how I got all of them. Maybe they didn't know how many I had. Maybe they thought I bought them with my lawn cutting money.

Dad had built a play house in our basement with leftover paneling from the house addition and other scrap wood he had in the garage. He also reused old rusty nails pulled from reclaimed lumber. The old man said you couldn't tell the difference when they were hammered flat, they held as good as new nails.

Wren, Coby, and I played in it all the time. As other kids do, we played house, but usually our games were more salacious. We often fooled around and played doctor. But we didn't peek into each other's eyes, ears, and throats. We kissed each other's butt cheeks instead. Wren played along with Coby and me, watching us do things to each other, while pretending to take our temperature and blood pressure.

A boy at school said, "Hey Kubacki, I heard you *couche* with your sister."

I had never heard the word before but I knew what he meant. My face flushed and I told the kid he was full of shit. Was he joking around with me? Like calling someone a mother fucker. Or did he know? Maybe Coby had told him something.

One day, my next-door neighbors, the Fosters, caught Coby and I playing doctor on the front lawn. We were lying under the aluminum awning that shades our living room. Looking out the window from the living room you could see Muriel at her sink washing dishes in the evening. The patch of lawn where Coby and I were fooling around was in clear view of the sidewalk and the street. Anyone nearby could have seen us.

Mrs. Foster came from her backyard, saw us,

looked away, and went inside the house. A few minutes later she came outside with her husband, Fitz. They walked toward us. Mrs. Foster picked up our clothes, handed them to us, and helped us get dressed.

Mr. Foster said, "What are you boys doing?"

Coby said, "Playing doctor."

"Yeah, playing doctor, Fitz."

"Oh, I see. It's only natural, you know. Boys will be boys. But this is something you should take inside."

Wren, Coby, and I also liked playing Truth or Dare. Coby and I dared each other to do things while Wren usually chose revealing a truth. But Coby and I didn't want to answer deep questions and she didn't want to poke her fingers into body cavities. The more physical things became, the less she wanted to play, and eventually, she stopped playing with us.

But Coby and I kept on playing.

"Truth or dare?"

I said, "Truth."

"What girl do you like at school?"

"Ask me something else, or I'll take a dare instead."

"Okay. I dare you to pull down your pants and underwear."

I did it, but also took off my socks and t-shirt.

I stood there stark naked. "Truth or dare?"

"Dare."

"I dare you to take off all your clothes."

After he stripped the game turned into something else.

He said, "Pretend you're sucking a Popsicle." And after that, he wiggled it around *where the sun don't shine,* trying to get it in.

We used to pull each other behind our bikes up and down South Street in the little red wagon. Sometimes, we towed each other on a skateboard, the skater holding onto the bike seat. We liked jumping our bikes and skateboards over improvised ramps, street curbs, and driveway easements.

At around nine years old, Coby got a new snowmobile and we wanted to do stunts with the new machine. We couldn't figure out how to make a ramp in the snow and decided dragging each other on the toboggan would be fun.

Coby, Zajac, and I made a path, driving around in circles to flatten out the weeds in the field. We removed a few big stones poking through the snow and threw them on a rockpile at the edge of the ditch. We made the path smooth and safe to drive fast as hell and pull the toboggan behind Coby's snowmobile. After about a half hour, Zee came up with something to make it more interesting.

"Why don't we try it without the sled?"

Coby and I agreed.

Coby took off dragging Stosh and me through the snow while we held onto the rear bar. After a few laps we switched drivers. We made a competition to see who could hang on the longest. If you fell off too soon, the other two called you a slacker, a sissy, or even worse, a faggot. *If you let go before the other guy, you're gay.*

Sometimes when Coby and I rode alone, after getting hot and sweaty, we stopped for a rest in the woods. He'd parked the snowmobile somewhere secluded, turn off the engine, and try to get inside my butt again.

One cold winter day, he succeeded.

Three

There's a lot of pests even on a clean and well-organized farm. Even though Grandpa Booms's grain bins were well maintained and dry they still had a few rodents to deal with in the barn. Setting traps caught a lot of field mice, and thankfully, they never had to deal with rats. But the worst vermin problem was the birds. European starlings. The damn starlings made nests in any nook or cranny they could find. When a bunch of them flew into the barnyard they gathered in the holding pen and holding lot and pestered the cows. That's why Uncle Bob and Ken had a BB gun. One afternoon, Bobby taught me how to shoot it.

"Now, close your right eye. Is the target still there?"

"No."

"Okay, close your left eye. Is the target there now?"

"Yeah."

"That means your right eye dominant."

"What does that mean?"

"It means you'll shoot aiming with your right eye while keeping your left eye closed."

"That makes sense."

Uncle Bob instructed me on the finer points of marksmanship. He showed me how to line up the front bead between the two beads at the rear. If the target was far away you raised the barrel to compensate for the distance. If it was a little farther than that you raised it even more. If it was windy outside you shot into the wind. You experimented to find the right trajectory. With practice it all becomes second nature.

My uncles liked to shoot at empty beer bottles and old coffee cans lined on top of a fence behind the barn. There were tons of brown bottles and several tin cans on the fence. Broken pieces of glass laid everywhere littering the ground.

I aimed carefully at the target and hit it. Glass tinkled to the ground.

"That's it. Just like that."

After a short while, I had had enough practice. We went hunting.

Bob cocked the gun, raised it up, and shot at a starling perched above a light. The bird flew away. A cloud of dust lifted into the air. We moved on and found another bird. This one was sitting quietly on a fence rail. Two more landed next to it. Bob aimed, zinged the center one, and it fell down without a sound. We walked around the property looking for more of them. Looked by the chicken coop, around the perimeter of the barn, and near the corn crib at the edge of the lane.

Just then we saw Uncle Ken walking down the lane behind the cows and Tippy. The rugged little dog was chasing the bovines. He ran under and around a cow's legs, barking, and nipping at the cow. It didn't matter if he got kicked in the face a few times, Tippy owned those heifers. My uncles began to call the cows while the dog did its work.

Ken hollered, "Coboss!"

Bob joined in, "Coboss."

And I followed suit, "Coboss."

"Coboss."

"Coboss."

"Coboss."

Tippy led the cows down the lane into the barnyard. Bobby and Kenny had to go milk the cows. Bobby asked if I wanted to help or keep hunting starlings. *What do you think I said?* He gave the gun to me, said, "Be careful with this," and I went hunting by myself. Shooting a few starlings would be easy and I was helping out by keeping the pesky birds out of the barn.

Walking down the lane I looked around the corn crib again. There were birds everywhere. They had followed the cows walking in from the field and took the opportunity to snag bugs stirred up by the cattle. Cocked, aimed, and fired, but nothing happened. I had completely missed and only scared the fucking birds away. Walking down the lane, around the corner at the rear of the barn, I went into the holding pen. The cows waited there until they were led into the milking parlor. In the parlor, they're hooked up to barrel milkers while the ladies enjoy a good meal and refuel their four-chambered stomachs. Afterwards, they were let into the holding lot by the water trough.

My uncles were busy inside feeding the cattle. Bob was up in the hayloft throwing feed down to Ken. Ken was in the aisle between the calf pens and a row of stanchions, scooping and distributing chow to the girls, stirring sweet dust into the air from the straw and hay.

For several minutes I saw nothing move. Then a big starling landed on a window ledge in front of me. I shot and missed. The glass pane shattered making a percussive clank. The breaking glass sounded good and I liked seeing it crack, splinter, and crumble to the ground.

I shot out another windowpane for the hell of it.

I walked around the barnyard toward the workshop. Near the scrap pile, I shot the mirror of an old rusty truck, shot out the window, and made some satisfactory dings in one of its hubcaps. Walking behind the shop, I realized I'd never been back there before. I went in to check it out.

Here there was a narrow alley between the shop and the lot. It formed a small rectangular area between the buildings, silos, and the holding lot – an empty space with nothing in it but weeds. I stood in the small court looking at the cows waiting for a turn at the water trough. The stupid cows were the reason I was out here hunting starlings. I was fed up with shooting birds and there was a cow right in front of me. Stupid fucking cow!

I raised my gun and shot her in the rear flank. It didn't flinch. I shot another animal in the shoulder. Shot at a couple more cows and none of them reacted. They stared with blank looks, mooing at me. I shot one in the teats. Her milk bag undulated, but no reaction. Nothing. Stupid cows. Goddamn stupid cows! I kept shooting them. After a while, one of them seemed to notice me. It walked over to see what *the stupid human was doing.* I think it wanted to talk to me. She looked at me with sadness in her eyes and said nothing. I shot it in the head, right between the eyes, and you know what? The damn thing didn't even blink.

Through the dirty barn windows Uncle Ken had seen me pop it in the face. He came marching down the parlor, opened a big sliding door, and tramped through the deep manure.

"What do you think you're doing?"

"I'm hunting starlings, Uncle Kenny."

"That's not what I saw."

"I was shooting at a bird. It landed right on the cow's back."

"Don't sweet-talk me, smarty pants, I saw what you were doing. Give me that gun."

He took the gun out of my hands.

"Go inside and think about what you did."

I said, "Okay," and walked toward the house.

"You ought to know better than that."

Kenny slogged back through the muck and went into the milking parlor to finish his chores.

When he was out of sight I walked to the shop. The huge sliding door was open. Warm air rushed out and carried dank smells of lubricating grease and welding slag. I walked inside.

A huge tractor and a gravity wagon sat in front of me.

I climbed into the tractor cabin and sat at the wheel pretending to drive. I got out of the cabin, walked to the wagon's inspection ladder, climbed up, got inside the bin, slid down the smooth steel sides, and curled into a ball at the bottom.

You stayed there, motionless, trying not to breathe, barely moving, until the large shop door came crashing shut. It was those men from the big red barn. You came back from where you were and realized you had been in that grain wagon for a long time. It was probably an hour or more.

Coby said, “I dare you to run naked outside.”

“Okay, but you’ve got to do it too.”

Coby took off his clothes and left them on the basement floor by his dripping wet snow suit and boots. I stripped down. We scrambled to the top of the stairs and ran outside into the brisk air.

My chest tightened in the cold air. We ran in the snow, around and around in circles, in the small yard between the garage and house. I picked up a handful of snow and threw it at him. We made snowballs and threw them at each other. The snow was wet and packed well. We flopped on our backs and made snow angels while singing a bad parody of *Jingle Bells.* Laughing our asses off, we jumped up from the ground, brushed the snow from our arms and legs, and ran into the house.

Before we had a chance to get dressed, Coby dared me to put my dick between the freezer box and door. He lifted the lid up to show me he was serious. Both of us put our dicks on the edge of the chest and carefully, ever so carefully, closed the door. We stood there with our hard dicks pressed under the magnetic gasket. Hearing a noise outside, we pulled out and quickly threw on our clothes.

I ran to the top of the stairs and looked out the frosty window of the back door. No one was outside. There weren’t any tire tracks in the driveway or foot-prints on the sidewalk. I went back downstairs. Coby was rummaging around in the freezer for something to eat.

“There’s nothing good in there.”

“You guys don’t have any Popsicles or ice cream? My mom keeps Fudgesicles in our basement freezer.”

“Nope, only a bunch of raspberries and a side of beef.”

“Have you ever climbed in and shut the door?”

“No. Are you kidding? It’s too cold in there. Besides, you could suffocate.”

“No, you wouldn’t.”

“But we saw it in that movie at school.”

“That only happens with old freezers, the ones with locking handles.”

“And old refrigerators.”

“Well, yeah. But this freezer doesn’t have a lock.”

“All right, I’ll try it, but you have to do it first.”

“Okay. I’m going to hold my breath while I’m in there, you time me.”

He took off his clothes.

“What are you doing?”

“Getting in the freezer.”

“Naked?”

“Yeah, we were naked outside. What’s the difference? Time me and then I’ll time you.”

“Okay.”

He got into the freezer and I shut the door. After a long time, it seemed like forever, he lifted the door gasping for breath.

He burst out laughing, “I’m only kidding!”

“Stop goofing around, Coby.”

He got out and put on his clothes.

“Now, it’s your turn.”

I stripped down and climbed into the chest. Getting down low, I tucked into a ball, and Coby shut the door.

The box darkened as the light turned off and everything went black as the door sealed shut. My butt cheeks stuck to a package of T-bone steaks. My senses dulled in the darkness. I waited as long as possible. Started shivering, quaking, and couldn't take it anymore. I pushed the door up and sprang out of the freezer.

Coby grabbed my arms and helped me out of the box. I sat for a moment on top of the big oak desk and put on my clothes.

"How long was I in there?"

"A minute and twenty-three seconds. I beat you by nine seconds."

Shutting the lid, I said, "Okay, you win."

Dad wanted to build a new tool shed and had sketched a plan for a small hip roof barn. Wanting a rustic look, he said we could reclaim lumber from his family's old barn in Ubly. We drove to the farmstead to see what we could get. *It was his childhood home* and he figured we could go there and *take the wood.*

Dad thought the house would be empty, but when we got there someone was renting the place. My old man chatted with the folks and told them he grew up in the house and talked his way inside for a tour. The people living there had let it go to hell. There was a lot of newspaper and debris strewn on the floor. It looked like an enormous hamster lived there. The crap rose partway up the walls. A lot of fancy glass knobs were missing from the doors and several hardwood floor planks had been removed.

Behind the house, we found the chicken coop filled with old empty cans and glass bottles, piles of it, two or three feet high. We took a look in the barn. A small pile of fresh garbage had accumulated in the cattle pens and grain silo. There were rats the size of opossums crawling in the trash.

We couldn't go tearing boards out of the barn with someone living there, so Dad thanked the people, we got in his rusty green F-100, and drove away. We went to the house next door, Dad's uncle's old place, about a hundred yards away. Like *Busia* and *Dziadzo,* he had also moved into Bad Axe for his retirement. There were renters and squalor there too. Since the barn had collapsed, we decided to tear off all the wood we needed and took home a pile of wide planks.

Dad had a lot of stuff in the garage that we needed for the project, old bent nails, two-by-fours, and partial sheets of plywood. For the foundation, we took four railroad ties from a pile beside the tracks near the grain elevators at the east end of town. We needed some more framing lumber, a set of three hinges, a padlock, and a hasp. We went to the lumber yard, picked up some more two-by-fours, some two-by-sixes and loaded it into Dad's truck. Now, we had to make a trip to the hardware store downtown.

I checked out the sleeping bags, tents, and other camping gear while he got what we needed. Near the cash register they had a big knife case locked on the bottom with a long piano hinge at the top. There was an even bigger glass cabinet filled with shotguns, rifles, and handguns. All locked up tight.

I hadn't shot a firearm before, not even a .22 caliber rifle, but I was quite interested in air guns and wanted a BB gun of my own. In the display case, I saw a CO2 pistol and a CO2 rifle next to the firearms, but no regular BB guns. Then I saw another display of guns laying on a low shelf behind the counter. A stack of BB guns, unlocked, sitting on the shelf. Brand new ones with a shiny polished wood handles and glimmering brass rivets. They had a pump-up gun, exactly like the one I wanted.

Of course, they had a cheap crank gun, but the pump-up one cost more. I would have to save money from a few lawn mowing jobs to buy the better one. I didn't think I could do it because Mom and Dad were always saying, "That money's going to burn a hole in your pocket." And they were right.

I snapped out of my daze when Dad said, "You ready, Steve?"

"Almost. I'm still looking at BB guns. I want to get one, Dad. Will you buy one for me?"

"Not today. Maybe some other time, sunshine. I'll have to talk it over with your mother first."

He put his items on the counter, paid the cashier, and we left.

I couldn't save money. I had never been able to save money and wouldn't be able to save a penny for this gun. *But I wanted it so badly!* Mom and Dad probably wouldn't buy it for me. No way. So, I decided to steal it.

I came back the next day to rip-off the gun. I had been stealing for a while now and knew how to take things without anyone noticing. But this thing was huge, I couldn't hide it in my clothes. I would have to go behind the counter when the cashier was busy, grab the BB gun, and walk out before anyone saw a thing.

I looked around for about half an hour. Two clerks asked if I needed any help. I told them I was just looking. The woman running the cash register would not leave the counter. When she wasn't ringing up a customer she stared out the window watching traffic. She was probably supposed to be dusting shelves or sweeping the floors, but she stood there, blocking access to my gun. There wasn't anything I could do. I couldn't pull it off.

"Thanks, have a good day."

"Thank you for coming in."

I walked out the front of the store and went into Murphy's Bakery next door. Small brass bells rang as the door opened. The aroma of earthy bread and a thick sugary mist wafted into my nose. I bought a long, custard filled doughnut smothered in chocolate icing and ate it on my way back home.

When I got home, I was still thinking about stealing the gun. How could I possibly take it? Maybe I *could* save up and buy the thing. But who was I kidding? Even if I could save the money I couldn't wait that long for the gun. I had to have it now. I decided to take some money from Dad's wallet, go downtown, and buy the damn thing.

Dad was outside tilling the garden and Mom was walking behind him picking up rocks and smoothing out the soil with a rake. I watched for a minute from the patio window as they started setting out strings to plant a row of seeds. They had a whole garden to plant.

I knew they would be busy all afternoon.

I walked into their bedroom, picked up Dad's wallet, and took out two twenty-dollar bills. I stuffed the money into my front pocket, folded the wallet shut, and placed it back in the spot where I had found it with the word Alaska facing up.

Rode my bike down the block to the hardware store, smiling all the way. I entered and walked directly toward the guns and knives, picked up the pump BB gun, and waited at the cash register. One of the clerks came over.

"Can I help you?"

"Yeah, I came in here yesterday with my dad."

"I remember. You're one of Bucka's kids."

"Yep."

"Well, how can I help?"

"Dad and I were looking at this BB gun." I set it on the counter. "I came back to buy it today."

"Okay, that's great. Where's your dad? Is he with you?"

"No, but I've been saving up. I've got enough money to buy it myself."

"Oh, okay."

"Can you ring me up?"

I handed the money to him, but he didn't reach for it. He picked up the gun and set it behind the counter.

"Your money's no good here, young man, at least not today."

"Why not? What do you mean?"

"I'm sorry son. I know you probably worked hard saving up to buy that BB gun, but you've got to be eighteen to purchase one in the State of Michigan. I can't let you buy it. Your eighteenth birthday has to be on or before today's date." He looked over his shoulder and pointed at the sign on the wall.

I kept the forty bucks and spent it on junk food.

At Christmas, I asked for a BB gun.

I knew how to work one safely, had a good eye, and every time we visited Grandma's house, I practiced shooting. But I would be a better shot if I had my own gun at home. I kept asking Mom and Dad for the gun but they didn't get me one for Christmas. But I kept pestering them. *Why wouldn't they buy me a BB gun?*

Near the end of May, I had forgotten about the gun. The school year was ending. All that was left was the rush of ditto paper tests smeared with blue ink and an ice cream social to kick off the summer. I couldn't stop thinking about summer vacation. Playing in the woods, riding bikes everywhere, and joining the reading club at the library.

Earlier that year, I had started playing chess and thought I was good at it. But somehow Mom beat me every time without reading the book on how to play. I wasn't too surprised on my birthday when I got a folding chess board with four-and-a-half-inch, solid plastic Kings. My parents also gave me a long thin package. I could tell *by its shape* what was inside. Tearing off the paper, I soon realized that it wasn't what I thought. It wasn't the BB gun, but a large piece of cardboard covered with red and white graphics, arranged in concentric circles, carefully designed to hold and display a bow and six arrows.

"This is so cool. It's not the BB gun I wanted, but this is great. Thanks for the archery set Mom and Dad. I love it!"

"Happy Birthday, Steve."

"We hope you like it."

"Yeah! This is really neat."

With my new bow and arrow, I could practice shooting anytime, and sure as shit, I still shot birds with Bobby's BB gun at the farm every Sunday.

Uncle Bob's several years older than me. He showed me all kinds of things that would've upset Mom and Grandma. Bob taught me how to reach the lowest rung of the silo inspection ladders. The trick is climbing up the huge hoops which hold the silo together. Using hand grips like a rock climber you scale the retaining rings up to the ladder and then climb it to the inspection platform.

Bobby let me into the milking parlor one time when a cow gave birth. My other uncles didn't want a young kid there watching a calf come into the world, especially this time, a breech birth, because the heifer needed help from the men. They used a strong rope tied around the calf's legs to pull it out while the cow pushed. I got to help pull the rope! We had a tug-of-war with the momma cow until the calf fell onto the floor and bellowed out, "Moooaaww!"

Grandpa must've liked having such a handy kid around the farm. Bobby was always mending fences, replacing rotten boards, and painting the barn and sheds. In 4-H he built good quality furniture. Glued, joined, and sanded in the workshop. He built beautiful pieces and always finished his work, without a single flaw, in a dark walnut stain and a thin coat of varnish on top.

Bobby helped plant and harvest crops, raise cows and chickens, and also had his own rabbits. The Boomses didn't name their milking cows and chickens and they didn't name their bunnies either. Like the other livestock on the farm, I knew these rabbits were for food.

Dad kept rabbits in our back yard behind the shed where nosy neighbors wouldn't see them. But a lot of people in town knew and came over often to see them anyway. Dad housed his rabbits in wood hutches with attached outdoor cages.

Uncle Bob had a lot more room on the farm to raise his brood. He took over Grandma's small chicken coop to keep his rabbits. Sometimes, Grandma kept baby chicks in the little coop to isolate them from full-grown hens, but it had been vacant for a long time and Bobby decided to use it.

There were gaps in the old chicken wire outside the small building. Chickens weren't too bright and they couldn't escape, but an inquisitive rabbit would find the holes in the fence. We plugged them with pieces of scrap wood and hardware cloth. We also closed two sliding hatches and nailed them up tight, but didn't secure the center pophole to give the rabbits access to the outdoor pen.

When the mess got out of hand, Bobby and I used a flat shovel and a pitchfork to scoop up the rabbit droppings and the urine-soaked straw. We composted the manure and spent bedding in Grandma's raspberry patch like Dad did at home with his rabbit shit in our garden.

One day during chores, Bobby asked me to help feed and water the rabbits. I flipped the stray turds out of the metal food bins, topped off the chutes with pellet food, and filled their water bowls. The rabbits needed some fresh air, so I opened the center pophole and secured the latch. I was watching as they ran outside through the tiny doorway when something happened. I hadn't placed the locking pin correctly or maybe I bumped the door. I'm not sure what happened, but the hatch fell. It fell onto one of the baby bunnies and snapped its neck.

I killed the wabbit. Poor little wabbit.

Bob tried to console me and placed a hand on my shoulder as I cried.

"It's okay, Steve, it was an accident. These things happen. Why don't you go inside? I got to help Kenny with chores in the barn."

You walked down the narrow sidewalk to the house. But instead of going inside, you walked towards the workshop, down the lane past the junk pile to the silos. You climbed to the top of one, sat cross-legged on the metal platform and stared, with spaced-out eyes, at the deep blue water of Lake Huron.

One dusty summer afternoon, we went to visit Grandma and Grandpa Booms. As the car rolled into the driveway, I was leaning out the car window ready to jump from the car before it stopped. I was full of piss and vinegar from thinking about camp the next day. We saw Grandpa walking in the field. The ground was strewn with scattered bits of debris from a recently harvested navy bean crop.

Mom said, “Hi Dad.”

Grandpa looked at Mom and said, “Hello, Charlie. The well’s gone dry. How’s the family doing today?”

Grandpa Booms used two wells to provide enough water for the house, but they often had to share bath water to keep from running out. Grandma didn’t use modern appliances, which wasted water, for washing laundry or doing dishes. She had a wringer washer and clotheslines for the laundry and washed and dried dishes by hand. One year, she made her kids return the dishwasher they had given her for Christmas.

Grandpa’s third well, for the cattle, was going dry. Some days there wasn’t a drop in the barn to wash the milkhouse. Fortunately, the water trough for the cows in the holding lot was still full of water.

I noticed Grandpa had a purple and green Y-shaped elder maple branch in his hands.

“What are you doing Grandpa?”

“Looking for water,” he said, gurgling, whistling, chomping at, and relighting his pipe. *I was thirsty You gave me to drink.* He showed us how the thing worked. It would show you where water was by pointing to a stream flowing underground. You walked back and forth in one direction, turned ninety degrees and walked the other way. Making a grid, like a checker-board, watching for the wand to move. Every now and then I noticed the branch bending and pointing to the ground as Grandpa walked.

Wren said, "Grandpa, can I try it?"

He gave the wand to her. She walked back and forth in a grid, the same area Grandpa had covered, but the stick didn't move.

"You want to give her a try?"

"No thanks, Grandpa."

"Go ahead, give it a try."

He handed the branch to me. I looked at it, took it, and held it like he had shown us. *Why not try it? It couldn't possibly work.*

I started walking in the checkerboard pattern. When I approached a spot where Grandpa had placed a good-sized field stone – one big enough to stone the martyr, St. Stephen – the damn thing bent towards the ground. I held the twig tighter but the branch resisted my grip, twisted in my hand, and the bark tore loose from the wood. When I passed Grandpa's stone marker the twig relaxed and straightened out again.

"He did it, Mom!"

"What just happened?" I couldn't believe it worked. *What the hell just happened?*

Grandpa placed two more stones next to the other one and went to the barn. The family went inside to see Grandma and I went looking for starlings. Needed to practice my aim for the archery range at Boy Scout camp tomorrow.

Grandpa Booms is a twin. Like many identical twins, a lot of people had a hard time telling the difference between Bernard, my grandpa, and his brother, Leonard. When they were kids, their older sisters had painted a single toenail pink on one of the boys to tell them apart. Maybe it was a finger nail, nobody remembers now. It doesn't matter, the ingenious system worked, and it worked well, until the lacquer washed off during their bath one day. Their sisters noticed it was gone after drying the boys off. The family stood them side-by-side, to get a better look, and *cast votes* to decide which boy was which. Did they choose correctly? Maybe they got it backwards and Uncle Leonard is really my grandpa, and Grandpa Booms is actually my great uncle. Only God knows for sure.

When we got home, I couldn't stop thinking about camp the next day. It was late. Dad was watching the eleven o'clock news, and Mom was setting the alarm on the clock radio. She walked us kids to the far end of the house to put us to bed. She tucked the girls in. Mom came into our room as I was pulling the blanket up to my chin. She kissed Jake and me.

"Goodnight, Steve. Goodnight, Jacob." We said goodnight to her. "Come here and say goodnight to the kids, Buck."

"Just a minute, dear, I've got to piddle." With the bathroom door open he finished urinating, walked into the hallway, and stood outside the bedrooms. He looked through the girl's door and then ours. "Goodnight, Wren. Goodnight, Tessa. Good night, boys."

Mom turned off the hall light and they walked to the other side of the house. Dad finished watching the eleven o'clock news on the boob tube and Mom went to bed.

I stayed awake for a while as cool night breezes came in through the window. I couldn't sleep because my thoughts were wrapped up in tomorrow. A hike in the woods, the archery range, swimming. The camp was going to teach us how to properly identify poison ivy and poison oak. Oh yeah, and canoeing. But the best thing would be shooting on a real archery range with proper long bows and perfectly straight arrows with sharpened tips.

If I slept at all, it was only for a short while. I woke, what felt like minutes later, to Dad shaking my arms and tapping me on the chest. He pulled down the blankets and grabbed my hands as I reached up to him.

"It's time to get up, sunshine."

I got out of bed, washed my face, wet my hair, mopped off with a towel, and dragged a comb across my head.

Mom had set out my Boy Scout uniform. I put on the dark blue outfit and yellow kerchief. I admired myself, the uniform, and the merit badges in the mirror. They reminded me of Dad's old Army badges and medals that he kept in a yellow margarine tub inside the top drawer of his dresser.

I went to the kitchen and ate a bowl of Cocoa Wheats with lots of sugar and peanut butter to make it taste better. I also ate two pieces of peanut butter toast dipped in the hot cereal, drank a small glass of orange juice and two big glasses of skim milk to wash it all down.

Mom walked in as I finished breakfast and said, "It's time to go."

Dad gave me a kiss on the cheek. His 100-grit sandpaper beard bristled against my face. He adjusted the belt on his bathrobe and went back to bed.

Mom drove to the junior high where the buses were

waiting. She parked the burgundy Cordoba. Getting out of the vehicle, I dodged her hugs and kisses. She said, "Have-fun-be-careful-I-love-you-we'll-see-you-tonight," as I ran away to find my buddies. Then she hollered, "Drink lots of water, it's going to be muggy."

I climbed into the big yellow bus. The driver asked my name and checked it off his list. A bunch of popular boys were sitting in the front of the bus. I found a good spot in the rear. The guys I liked were back there. The den mothers and two den fathers sat chatting with the other chaperones, a few Eagles, and two older girls – sisters of a kid in my scout den.

The buses rolled out of town.

It was still early morning. The sun had not yet painted the sky pink. We sat staring out the windows waiting for silhouettes to appear in the horizon. Some guys were talking about the Tigers. How they would do this year, the star pitcher, that kind of crap. I tried my best to ignore them, kidding myself I didn't care, but I was jealous because I was lousy at sports.

Some of the boys were teasing another kid. The poor guy was *slow,* looked pale all the time, and had almond-shaped eyes. He came from a poor family and didn't have many friends. The boys heckled him and called him retard. The chaperones finally noticed and one of the den mothers came over and split it up. She separated the rowdy boys and seated each of them with their own personal chaperone. The poor kid stayed in his seat and the bullies left him alone.

Everyone settled in for the long ride. It became quiet and a lot of us dozed off while we travelled down the road. The bus driver opened a thermos and poured himself a cup of coffee while he steered the wheel with his left knee. Music was playing on the radio, volume turned low, barely audible above the hum of the bus rolling down the road. The smell of a new day came in through the open windows, a heavy humidity from the fields, air thick with pollen.

Almost everyone had fallen asleep and the driver probably had a glaze in his eyes as we pulled into a long gravel driveway and stopped with a screech in a parking lot at the edge of a woods. Everybody scrambled to grab their backpacks and other gear and we got off the bus. With only a day to spend at camp we were ready to go.

The camp leaders got our blood pumping by taking us on a long hike. It took about an hour. The walk was probably about a mile. The Eagle Scout leading us knew the trails well. He knew exactly where we were going in the woods. I was surprised when he reached for a map in his pocket and removed a lanyard compass from his neck. He set the map on the ground and laid the compass on top. He positioned the compass to align the needle with north on the map. I understood what he was doing right away, as did most of the other boys, but for a few of them the concept didn't click.

During the hike we learned to identify poison ivy, poison oak, and poison sumac. The simple phrase, *Leaves of three let it be,* doesn't work. Poison oak has three leaves but they are rounded and not pointy like poison ivy. Poison sumac has seven to thirteen leaflets and looks nothing like the other two poisonous plants. And then there's water hemlock – also known as cowbane, because cattle eat it, become violently sick, and often die – which looks like the wildflower, Queen Anne's lace. You need more knowledge of plants to be accurate and safe. The Eagle taught us about wetland plants like American bamboo, also known as the snake plant, and the beautiful flowering trillium. I already knew the basic leaf shapes of maples, oaks, willows and other common trees, but our guide showed us the subtle differences between species in each genus.

The most incredible thing we saw was the snake pit. The camp housed every native species of snake, reptile, and amphibian. They even had a massasauga, the poisonous Michigan rattlesnake with short, almost useless fangs, and no rattle.

At lunch we ate cafeteria style. There was nothing good to eat. I grabbed a tray and picked up a Faygo grape pop and a Hershey bar. The lodge mess hall was huge with a big stone fireplace in the middle of the room. Like at school, I wasn't sure where to sit and barely talked to anyone.

We couldn't dig into our food right away but had to wait until everyone was seated. When all were seated, nearly a thousand boy scouts, leaders, and chaperones bowed their heads and prayed together. While everyone in the massive room lowered their heads and said grace, I sat there listening, moving my lips but not uttering a single word.

We left the dining hall and walked to the edge of a lake formed by a dam on the Au Sable River to go swimming. I thought it was dangerous to be in the water after eating. You're supposed to wait an hour before swimming or you'll drown from stomach cramps, but they informed us it was an old wives' tale.

There was no locker room. They had set up eight poles with ropes tied between them. The three changing areas were made of white canvas tarps hung from ropes cinched at the corners of the half-assed construction. The canvas walls of the changing rooms ruffled in the steady breeze off the lake. I could see boys in the adjacent rooms as we stripped down to put on our swimming suits. The boys on one side were much older, they had thick pubic hair, big penises, and looked like grown men. On the other side, I could see into the younger boys changing area. I could also see the adults outside the tents which meant they could see us. *What the hell?*

Swimming was awkward because we had to use the stupid buddy system. You had to stay with your buddy to make sure no one drowned. Your buddy watched you and you watched him while you *tried to swim.* I couldn't swim worth a shit anyway. But, every couple of minutes the camp leaders shouted, "Buddies! Buddies! Everyone buddy-up. Buddy-up everyone." There was hardly any time to swim and we complained to each other about it. We wanted to swim, damn it! Screw the buddy system. Despite the awful restrictions, we had a good time swimming in the Au Sable and earned a merit badge for our scout uniforms.

Rowing a canoe, I earned another patch for my uniform. Some of the boys chose to use rowboats because they couldn't manage the canoes. All you had to do is row fifty yards in a straight line, make a few turns, paddle back to shore, and you earned the badge. I thought the canoe was easy to use and they were being sissies having to use a rowboat. Almost all the boys felt the same and we gave them a hard time about it.

"You faggot! You can't row a canoe?"

"Quit being a wuss! Get a real boat."

We spent a couple hours of the hot afternoon at the archery range. Nobody had to wait long for a turn because the camp had twenty professional targets with five or six people in each line. They showed us proper marksmanship techniques and how to string a long bow – which I already knew. At the end of the day, we sang silly songs and watched some bad skits.

On the way home everyone was quiet, speaking in whispers. Some of the boys were talking about cute girls they had seen at camp – teenage chaperones from other scout troops. They talked about their shapely legs, alluring smiles, long silky hair, and naturally, their big jugs.

I don't remember what led up to it or exactly how it played out. Was I showing off to the other boys? I don't know. But I let everybody on the bus know that not all guys liked big jugs. And to make things worse, I said something to the sisters of a scout in my den sitting nearby on the bus. His family attended my church. His parents and my parents played on the same bowling league.

But I did it. I said it. "Both of you girls have nice tits. Cami's boobs are bigger, but Judy's are smaller and perkier, and I like little titties more than big jugs!" The bus went completely silent.

It was a dull silent ride until we rounded the big curve on Van Dyke Road past the Pinnebog River bridge. After the road straightened out again, we could see the Ferris Wheel in the distance, brightly lit up on the glowing midway, far down Soper Road at the fairgrounds. Slowly, effervescently, the bus came alive with the excitement of chattering boys.

The fair was back in town!

After Coby's fort was tore down by Mr. Dreher for some reason, Wren and I wanted a fort in our back yard. Dad used three old cedar fence rails as legs under our fort. The fourth leg was a cut off branch of a living apple tree. The framing was quite simple and only had wall studs in the corners. Two walls were sheathed with plywood scraps, one wall was built from reclaimed wood siding, and the front wall was leftover barn wood planks from Dad's tool shed.

At first, there wasn't a door, only an opening in the front wall. Later, Coby and I installed a simple sliding door made from an old piece of plywood. We tacked teen idol pinups on the backside of the flimsy sliding door. When playing our dirty games in the fort, we lay down under posters of Farrah Fawcett and Cheryl Ladd, and we stared up at them as they stared down at us.

On the front of the fort Dad had built a small deck and cobbled together a ladder. One beautiful summer day, Coby and I were sitting on the tiny deck admiring apples we had lined up. A small leather cased transistor radio was playing AM Gold on the Detroit station CKLW.

"Do we have enough apples?"

"Yeah, I think we have enough."

We were climbing down the ladder when we saw two older boys coming up my neighbor's driveway. They continued to the end of the drive, stepped into the yard, ducked under Mom's clothesline, and came toward us as we climbed back on the deck. They trampled through the garden and kept coming toward us. Coby and I stood on the deck waiting for them.

I recognized them. It was Rolf and Eddie, two older kids from school.

Rolf said, "That's a cool fort, guys."

Eddie said, "Yeah, pretty cool."

"Who built it?"

"I did."

Rolf continued, "So, this is your place Kubacki?"

"Sure is."

Eddie said, "Can we check out your fort?"

"You already are."

"What I meant is can we come inside and have a closer look?"

"No."

Rolf said, "Well, it is a pretty cool fort. Emphasis on pretty."

"Screw you!"

"What did you say?"

"Fuck you is what he said!"

They stayed a few more minutes exchanging insults with us. After they had had enough, they turned around and walked back though the garden toward the street. As they got close to Dad's shed, I screamed at them, "Get the fuck out of here you assholes!" I picked up my bow, notched an arrow, aimed at the boys, and released it. As soon as the string snapped, I realized the mistake I'd made. It was sheer stupidity. Watching the arrow fly through the air I hoped it would miss, but it found its target and hit Eddie in the palm of his right hand.

"What the fuck!"

"What the hell happened, Eddie?"

"That fucking Kubacki kid shot me in the hand!"

"What the fuck, man?"

"Kubacki shot me in the goddamn hand."

Eddie clutched his hand trying to stop the bleeding. He and his buddy ran down the neighbor's driveway, slowed to a fast walk near the sidewalk, and crossed the street. They cut between two houses and ran out of sight.

A few hours later, a Michigan State Police cruiser pulled in and parked at the end of our driveway. A trooper in a dark blue uniform and an important looking hat got out of the car. He adjusted his brim, walked across the lawn, went up the front steps, and knocked on the door.

The heavy door opened with a swoosh and Dad poked his head out. He pushed the screen door open and let the cop into the foyer.

"Mr. Kubacki?"

"Yes, I'm Buckley Kubacki, and this is my wife, Charlene."

"Hello."

"I'm Officer Gleaner, Eddie's dad."

My dad gave the cop a blank look.

I wasn't expecting this, at least not this soon, but there he was, the man in blue, a State Trooper, *in my living room,* talking to Mom and Dad. The officer said he wasn't talking to them in an official capacity but told my parents what I had done to his son.

"Your kid shot Eddie in the hand with an arrow. It's nothing serious. That boy of yours must be one hell of a shot. I came by to talk to you in person, Buck. You know? Man-to-man."

"Uh, okay."

"Now that you know what happened, you know how to take care of him, don't you, Buck?"

"Oh yeah, I'll take care of him. He's full of piss and vinegar. *Jezus kocha mnie.*"

He said, "All right, I guess that settles it," satisfied Dad had got the message, but the cop's intimation had not registered at all.

After Officer Gleaner backed out of the driveway my parents scolded me for shooting an arrow at the kid.

"What the hell is wrong with you? We bought that bow for you to shoot at targets."

"Yes, Steve, your father's right."

My parents confiscated my bow, arrows, and quiver, but I talked them into giving it back within a week.

Four

Mr. Garner knew a farmer actively clearing his woods to make more arable land. He had a huge lot of poplar, aspen, and cottonwood, mixed with some good maple. Most of it was crappy firewood, but there were plenty of trees to cut down, and it was free.

Stan could run a chainsaw better than anyone in our group, so he cut down the trees. His kid, Billy, and I dragged the trees after Mr. Garner chopped them down. Bill backed up the small, gray Ford tractor while I guided him to the log. I attached a chain to the log, gave Bill a signal, and he pulled the tree to a clearing. In the clearing, my old man removed the branches and cut the timber into manageable pieces. When Stan finished cutting down trees, he helped my dad cut up the logs.

Mrs. Garner, Mom, and Wren stacked the wood and worked on cleaning up the mess. Even little Tessa collected small handfuls of twigs and carried them to the brush pile. Jake crawled around in the weeds, or sat near the brush pile, watching us work. The ladies kept an eye on him to make sure he was safe and stayed out of trouble. As the girls cleared the debris, Bill and I pulled more trees from the woods for our dads to cut up.

After all the timber was cut, the brush removed and piled up, we stopped to have lunch. Refreshed from a quick bite to eat we went back to cut some more wood.

The work was done after we filled two pickup trucks and a wagon pulled by the tractor. We did this every time we went to the woods and we went cutting nearly every weekend in the summer.

When my neighbors, the Koles, asked Dad for help, a small favor for the family across the street, Stan knew we would have no trouble cutting down their tree. Mr. Kole's old willow tree had gotten too damn big and it had to go. It had grown past the roofline of their sturdy two-story house. You could see it billowing over the rooftop from our living room window. We didn't measure it, but it must've been fifty-five or sixty feet tall, and four or four and a half feet wide. It was a big tree, a fucking big ass tree! We had processed hundreds of trees at La Bonne's farm. We could tackle this thing. It was only one goddamn tree.

Before starting the project, we moved Kole's picnic table, lawn chairs, and swing set to the back fence.

To be on the safe side, Stan thought the tree needed some help to fall in the right direction. He figured we could tie a heavy rope high in the tree, bind the rope to a chain, and attach the chain to the tractor.

Bill grabbed a rope from behind the tractor seat, handed it to me, and said, "Here you go, Stevie. I know you can do this."

My dad got an extension ladder for me to climb the massive tree. Stan and my dad leaned the ladder against the tree under the lowest branch. I tied the rope to my waist, climbed the ladder to the top, and I tied the rope around a big branch.

Bill walked to the tractor, unwrapped the chain from the hitch, and set it on the ground. He tied the rope to the chain and hopped onto the tractor seat. Bill rolled ahead until the line was off the ground but still had some slack.

Mr. Garner fired up his biggest saw, the sucker was

three feet long, and began cutting the tree. It took him a long time to cut the notch, a crucial step to make sure the tree fell in the right direction. A slight breeze blew, rocking the tree as he cut, and pinched the saw blade. Stan placed a wedge in the cut, hit the wedge with a sledge to open it up, and started cutting again. He took great care to finish the notch. When it was done, he removed the chunk of wood. He gave a signal to Bill who slowly released the clutch, inching the machine forward, until the chain and rope was taut.

Stan started the final cut on the opposite side of the notch. He told everyone to clear out of the area and yelled, "Get away from the tree!" We moved away and watched with anticipation as Mr. Garner cut the last band of wood from the behemoth. He shouted, "Look out!" But the tree didn't move an inch.

After a moment, the tree rotated on its detached stump and let out a loud croaking belch, an immense grating sound of wood on wood as the separate pieces of trunk ground into each other. The big ass tree started to lean the wrong way – towards Kole's house.

"Billy! Give her everything you've got!"

He revved the tractor engine, popped the clutch, and made two deep ruts in the lawn as the wheels spun around. The tires grabbed and the sudden forward momentum made the tractor pop a wheelie as the rear wheels dug deeper into the turf. The tree leaned closer to the house. Branches were pressing into the gable, tearing the shingles, drip edge, and facia from the peak of the roof. Mrs. and Mr. Kole stood watching, paralyzed. The tree moaned as it pivoted. Bill gunned the engine again, and the chain and rope vibrated like an oversized bass fiddle string.

The weeping willow stood motionless for a few seconds. All motion had stopped. Then the thing fell slowly away from the house. It was the slowest moving thing I'd ever seen. Mr. Kole was laughing and Mrs. Kole was wiping tears away from her eyes as it fell. Its dense foliage and graceful limbs looked like a giant green umbrella as it fell in the yard between two beautiful box elder maple trees.

The Koles pitched in to clean-up while Stan and Dad cut logs. My old man used one of Mr. Wilke's big saws. There was a lot of cutting to do, so Billy and I ran little chainsaws to help with the tons of tree limbs and brush. Some kids from the neighborhood, Coby, Stosh, and a few others, were recruited to carry armfuls of brush to clean up the yard. They had lots of fun helping us clean up the mess.

We cut down the big ass tree, damaged the Kole's roof, trim and siding, nearly destroyed their home, and Billy did a fantastic lawn job in their yard. But hey, no one got killed! Anyway, that's how neighbors help neighbors in Bad Axe, Michigan.

One hot summer day, I was rummaging through Mom's spice cupboard to find the Kool-Aid. She had the foil packets arranged by color. I found a yellow packet. Now I needed sugar.

I had seen a mail order ad in a comic book. *Send in cash, check, or money order to receive rare collectible coins by mail.* I had spent all of my money on junk food and didn't have any left to buy the coins. I needed to raise three dollars and forty-nine cents, plus forty-nine cents shipping and handling. I decided to earn the money by setting up a lemonade stand.

I opened the wood box and found only a smattering of white granules on the bottom of the bin. I looked in the brown sugar bin too, but there was nothing there either. *We had no sugar in the house.*

Mom was always running next door to borrow something, and Mrs. Foster often came over here asking for a cup of milk to bake a cake for Fitz. I knew I could get some sugar from her. I walked to her house and knocked on the side door. Muriel leaned over the stairs from the kitchen and saw me outside the screen door.

"Oh, it's you, Steve."

"Hi, Muriel. Is Fitz home?"

"He's in the den watching the Tigers."

"Tell him I said hi."

"All right, dear. Fitzgerald! Steve says hello."

He hollered from the den, "Hello, Steve!"

"Muriel, I'm setting up a lemonade stand. I've got nearly everything, but Mom doesn't have any sugar. I was wondering if I could borrow a cup."

She said yes, went to the cupboard, measured it, poured it into red plastic Coca-Cola cup, and handed it to me.

"Here you go, Steve. Good luck selling your lemonade."

"Thanks, Mrs. Foster."

I ran back home and borrowed some change from Dad's dresser. In the kitchen, I made a pitcher of lemonade with ice and put it in the fridge. Next, I went into Dad's shed, grabbed some leftover two-by-fours and plywood to build a small table. When the table was finished, I raised a pair of two-by-fours and nailed a plank between the uprights to advertise my business. Using old lavender paint from my bedroom I wrote on the sign.

Lemonade 10¢

I put the stand near the front sidewalk under the silver maple to keep me and the lemonade cool. Anticipating good business, I poured some lemonade into Tupperware cups and set them out for my customers. While waiting, I counted, and recounted the change in my empty cigar box. Fitz had given it to me. He was fond of smoking cheap drugstore cigars and had lots of the boxes in his garage.

A car drove by and honked its horn. Toot-toot.

A cute girl and her puppy walked past and said, "Hello."

An attractive lady and her thirsty kids waved as they passed by on their bikes.

I sat there in the shade. Waiting.

A door slammed shut. The noise startled me. I looked behind me and saw Mr. Foster crossing his driveway. Fitz walked into our yard, walked around to the front of the stand, and said, "Hello, Steve. How cold is your lemonade? It's quite a hot today. I hope it's really cold."

"It is, Fitz. I've got the coldest lemonade in town."

"All right then, I'll have a cup."

He gave me a quarter and I gave him his change. Fitzgerald stretched, picked up his cup, and casually sipped the drink.

"It's good."

"Thank you."

Mom and Muriel came into the yard as Fitz finished his beverage. He set the empty cup on the counter. The ladies walked around and stood in front of the stand. Mom ordered two and paid for both drinks.

I had earned another twenty cents to buy the rare coins I wanted. But after selling lemonade for an hour, I had earned only thirty cents for all my hard work, effort, *and investment.* I needed more customers to reach my goal.

The ladies finished their drinks and set down their cups. I put them under the table.

Muriel said, "That's good lemonade. Good thing you found some sugar."

"It's delicious, Stephen."

"It *was* the coldest in town."

As they walked away, I overheard Fitz say, "That boy's quite a businessman, Charlie." They all laughed at the witty comment and I smiled in spite of them. Fitz didn't, but might as well have said, "Low overhead, high profit."

I had more lemonade to sell.

A kid from school, Judd Farrow, rode up on his bike. He stopped, parked his ride, and walked to the stand.

"Is your lemonade any good?"

"Yep, it's the best in town. Ask any of my customers."

"Okay, I'll try a cup."

He placed a nickel and five pennies on the table. I picked up a clean glass and poured the yellow drink. Judd chugged it down in one big gulp.

"It's good, Kubacki."

"Thank you."

"Thank you! I've got to get going. I'll see ya at school, huh?"

"Yeah, I'll see ya later, Judd."

He got on his bike and rode away.

Sliding the coins off the table I noticed their dull patina. Looking closer, I realized what they were. Simply couldn't believe it, but there in my hand were four Indian head pennies, one World War II steel penny, and one Indian head buffalo nickel. *Holy crap!*

I picked up the pitcher and gulped down the rest of the lemonade. I dismantled the stand and put everything away. I had made forty cents *pure profit*, and this last sale was collectible coins – my goal in the first place. Success!

I went to my bedroom and got out my dark green coin binder. I wiped off the coins, trying not to burnish or polish them, and put them in the folder. I took the mail order form from my junk drawer, crumpled it into a ball, and tossed it in the trash.

The next day, a strange woman came to our house and knocked on the front door. She talked quietly to Mom for a few minutes, said goodbye, and then walked back down the sidewalk.

Mom yelled, "Stephen Mark!"

"Yeah, Mom."

"One of the boys from school – Judd – that was his

mom. She said you have something that belongs to them. Mrs. Farrow said you have some of her husband's coins. Judd took them off his father's dresser. That sounds like something right up your alley. Hm, hm, hm."

"Oh, that's what this is about? I've got the coins."

"Well, heck. You have to give them back, Stephen. You have to return them and make an apology."

"Apologize for what? It's not as if I stole them. Judd did."

"Stephen Mark."

I agreed with her and said I would take care of it.

I went to their house. I rode past the place every day going to school. After setting my bike down, I knocked on the door, and Mrs. Farrow answered. Judd was standing behind her. Mrs. Farrow said, "Thanks for coming over, Steve."

"You're welcome."

"Yeah, thanks Steve."

"Sure, Judd, sure."

"We're sorry about the misunderstanding. My husband loves collecting coins. He also collects stamps. He was looking at his coins today and noticed some missing. Well, we talked to Judd, and he told us what happened. We do appreciate you coming by."

They looked at me with glitter in their eyes. But their smiles faded as I explained. I sold a cup of lemonade to Judd, he paid me in cash, and where he got the coins was no concern of mine.

"I'm keeping the coins. They belong to me now."

I got on my bike and rode away.

I started collecting coins because Billy Garner had introduced me to the hobby. But Bill and I enjoyed talking about fish even more. We both kept fish tanks and liked to go fishing together because his old man and mine were usually too busy to bother. We fished a lot at the road commission gravel pit. There were plenty of big catfish and bass swimming around in the quarry.

I usually fished with Dad's push-button Zebco rod because it was easy to use. Bill used a spinner rod and reel or his little fishing thingamajig, the Ronco Pocket Fisherman. It folded down to the size of a small football. You pressed a button to open the rod like a switchblade, and it had a built-in tackle box too. When I tried using his spinner rod, I could never figure out how to flip the bail. When I flipped it the spool of line unraveled into a bird's nest. I gave up. I could catch more fish with my old man's fishing rod or the Ronco. We caught a lot of bluegill and crappie in the quarry. Garner even caught a huge largemouth bass covered in shades of silver and metallic green.

But one day we were under the one lane bridge on Nugent Road near his house. There were fish in the goddamn ditch. The fish must have swum all the way from Lake Huron, into the mouth of the Pinnebog, and past Mr. Banner's favorite fishing spot at the side of Grassmere Road where Wren fell into the river earlier that spring. My sister told me decades later about her experience.

I can still remember what I saw when I fell into the Pinnebog River. I was completely submerged. It felt like hours down there. Willow leaves were draped in the water and a green mist floated below the surface. It was strangely and startling beautiful. My green dress wafted away and back to me. Forever suspended, floating underwater. I felt terrified and at peace. Suddenly, a man's hand reached down and grabbed me. It was dad. He pulled me out of the current and sat me on a slippery rock on the bank. Chaotic noise crashed into my ears. When they got me back to Banner's house and dried me off, I had to wear Johnny Banner's jeans. How gross! A girl wearing boys' jeans.

The damned fish swam right past where my sister nearly drowned. They swam thirty-some miles up the river, through several more miles of water – a maze of farmer's drains and ditches – and wound up in this stream only to be caught by two bored punks on a hot summer afternoon.

Billy knew, but I didn't have a clue, we were fishing the Colona Drain. Back then, I didn't even know the ditch connected to the lake. Didn't know the concept of a watershed. Didn't know about dredging shallow brooks to create better drainage. I had no idea where the water drained and had no idea how fish got in the ditch. I didn't think or care about how they got there. *Maybe God put them there?*

We weren't having much luck with long rods. The water was too low. The Ronco worked well because it was compact and easy to use in the creek. But there weren't any big fish, all the big ones were in the Pinnebog and Lake Huron. But we kept trying for what seemed like hours. After we ran out of worms, Billy grabbed a landing net and set it on the bottom of the drain.

"What are you doing?"

"Changing techniques."

"Can we do that?"

"Nobody's going to see us out here."

A few minutes passed and he pulled up the net. It was full of fish. It was incredibly full of fish and we weren't sure what to do with all of them. Bill reached into the net and grabbed one. A catfish. It twitched violently and stung his hand with her long whiskers. He dropped the fish back into the net. "Stevie, would you fill that pail for me?" I dipped it in the creek, handed it to him, and he emptied the net into the green pail. We looked inside the bucket to see what else was in there. After a quick inspection we set the pail on a ledge under the bridge.

"We should get a bigger net."

"That's what I was thinking. But I've got an even better idea."

We went to his house and got three more green pickle pails from the garage. I waited in the shade of the garage while Bill walked to the pole barn. He came out a few minutes later balancing a rusty window screen on his head.

"Is that our net?"

"You got it!"

We went back to the bridge and walked down the grassy embankment to the water's edge. We put the five-gallon buckets on the bank and threw the screen into the center of the small stream.

We waited about five minutes and lifted the screen out of the water. *It was easy pickings.* A channel catfish shimmered iridescent pink, gray, and purple. The bluegills sparkled blue, aqua, tones of green, and were brushed with red, orange, and yellow. There was a small, silvery-green, largemouth bass, its sides marked with faint black stripes. We also caught a tiny yellow-bellied perch tipped with daubs of bright red. We sorted the fish by size. Bill took the big ones and I took the rest.

When Mom and Dad saw my new fish, they asked if I bought them downtown. "Nope. Bill and I caught them near Garner's house. Right down the road under the one-lane bridge." They thought it was neat that we had caught our own aquarium fish.

Did they even know what we had done is poaching?

That summer, the Garners hosted a cookout. It was one of their kid's high school graduation parties. After eating hot dogs, hamburgers, and Dad's rabbit – which he passed off as chicken to unsuspecting guests – we played a few innings of baseball.

Jacob loved playing ball and he was good at it too. He made a home run during the friendly scrimmage after a decent centerfield hit. With some help from the opposing team sandbagging he made it to home plate. Around the top of the sixth inning, we quit the game. The adults sat in lawn chairs and grumbled about their upset stomachs from overeating and the kids went inside to watch TV.

While we watched the idiot box Bill fed his fish. He fed the guppies, which were kept in a separate breeding tank, and removed the dead ones with a tiny net. After they were fed, he scooped a netful of guppies, carried the net to his fifty-gallon tank, and released them into the water.

The shiny green bass we had caught in the ditch exploded from the bottom of the tank, lunged to the surface, and sucked in a mouthful of guppies. A pod of bluegills swam around the bass eating the ones it had missed. The yellow perch came up from the bottom and joined the bluegills. A channel catfish and a few chubby corydoras catfish – the only tropical fish in the tank – joined the feeding frenzy and cleaned up the leftovers on the gravel bed.

Mr. Garner, my dad, and their buddies came into the house as Bill was dipping the net back into the feeder tank for more guppies. He transferred the net to the big tank to feed the predators again. After the feeding frenzy was over, Bill floated some pellet food on top of the water to make sure they had enough to fill their bellies.

"These fish look like the fish you have," my dad said, "but they're bigger than yours."

"I've got a lot of the same fish. Billy took the big ones and I took the rest."

"We caught them under the bridge down the road, Mr. Kubacki."

"From that ditch everybody sucker-fishes in the spring?"

"Yeah, the Colona Drain."

After watching Bill feed his fish, all the guys went upstairs to get away from the adults *and the girls.* We sat around trying to catch a cool breeze from the open window and a blast of air from an oscillating fan.

His bedroom was huge. It took up two thirds of the

upstairs in Garner's house. In one corner Bill had a large-scale train set up on sheets of plywood. He had painted it green with patches of brown and blue to suggest a landscape – no miniature villages or fake trees. He and his brother used the table as catchall for their keys, wallets, and other crap. The train set was cool, don't get me wrong, but you might as well forget it, because the best stuff on the tabletop were his collectibles. Billy had collections of rocks, coins, stamps, a bunch of car emblems, and some old pale green, clear, and blue glass electrical insulators.

Picking up a rusty chrome emblem I said, "Where did you get these?"

"Most of them are from junkyards."

"They're so cool."

Billy was three years older than me and he lived three miles from my house. The Garners lived a short way out of town near the Bad Axe airport. I could ride my bike to his house in about twenty-five minutes, thirty-five if I was taking my time. Sometimes, Bill would come into town and we went riding on the trails behind my house.

One hot summer day, we were riding the trail to the fairgrounds. Dust and pebbles popped out from under our wheels as we rode through the woods. The fair had packed up the week before but we could always find something to do even if the fair was over. The horse barns were always open. A lot of riders kept their animals at the fairgrounds all year. Usually, someone was around taking care of their horses, feeding and watering them, currying down their coats, inspecting their shoes for wear and tear. But no one was in the barns that afternoon. I told Billy that my neighbor Mike kept his horse in one of the barns. We went to Mr. Braeburn's stall and gave Little Mike a few handfuls of oats. I scooped up a pile of turds and threw them into a dusty wheelbarrow. We walked through the stables to look at the other horses and stopped to check out the Sheriff's horse before leaving the barn.

Trash pickers had not yet cleaned up the midway. The litter barrels were overflowing and the garbage had spilled onto the ground. We walked into a tent left standing by a vendor but there was nothing inside. A miniature silo had been built on site that year, I had wanted to climb it, but couldn't do it during the fair. Bill and I climbed it that afternoon. We figured it was twenty-five feet tall. Half the size of Grandpa Booms's silos.

Some farm equipment was still parked in the long grass. We got on one of the tractors. Billy sat in the driver's seat and I sat on the rear fender.

"This tractor would be great for hauling wood."

"This *is* a great tractor."

"It sure is, Stevie."

Bill fiddled with the shifter, traced the gear pattern, and worked the hydraulic levers. He unscrewed one of the knobs and put it in his pocket, then removed another knob and handed it to me.

"You want one?"

"We can take it?"

"How do you think I got all those car emblems? *I swiped 'em.*"

"Cool."

Early that fall, one day after school, Mason Kole and I were playing on the swing set in his back yard. We were swinging back and forth when the set's legs started lifting off the ground. I vaulted out of my seat before it tipped over, flew through the air, and landed flat on my ass. Mason waited for the motion to stop before getting off his swing.

I brushed off the seat of my pants and we walked to the back fence. We stood there looking into the neighbor's back yard.

"Whose car is that? I haven't seen it before."

"It's my new neighbor's. He just moved in."

"It's so cool."

I don't remember what kind of car it was, but it was big, shiny, and black. It reminded me of the Satellite my old man bought when he was home from Alaska on leave from the Army. The owner of this car had put a lot of work into it. The paint and chrome trim were well polished and the front fenders had the coolest emblems I'd ever seen. They said V-8-4.

It doesn't matter if a car has a 305, or a big ass 454, as long as you had an eight-cylinder engine you're going to move fast. Those old muscle cars were paired up with the right engine at the factory, but if you had to have more horsepower you could always put in an oversized crankshaft, a bigger camshaft, and bore out the block.

Mrs. Kole yelled from the back porch, "Mason Kole! Get in here and take care of these dogs! Socks and Boots need food and fresh water."

While Mason fed his dogs, I hopped over the fence into the neighbor's yard. Using my penknife, I popped an emblem from the driver's side fender and put it in my pocket. I climbed back over the fence into Kole's yard. Mason finished feeding the dogs and came outside.

"It's almost supper time. I have to go home. See ya later, Mason."

"Okay Steve, see ya later."

A couple of days later, a strange man showed up at our house, knocked on the front door, and asked for me. I sat on the back stairs listening while Mom spoke to him. He said I had stolen an emblem from his classic car. There's no way Mason or his mom saw me. There are too many shrubs along the back fence. The man probably saw me climbing into his yard. I knew I was in trouble.

I walked through the living room toward the front door, rummaged in my pocket, extended my hand and said, "Here's your emblem, sir. I'm sorry about taking it."

"Thank you, young man." He gave me a vague smile and explained how parents should keep a better eye on their kids, and then with the same breath, he asked who would pay for the damages.

"What damages? The car is in perfect shape. I didn't damage the car at all."

Mom looked back and forth between the man and me.

He said he would have to touch-up the fender after the repair and then wax the entire car to maintain its uniform finish. He looked Mom in the face and asked again who would pay for the repairs.

"I'm not going to pay for it. He can work it off."

The man reluctantly agreed to Mom's suggestion.

I was supposed to mow the man's back yard five or six times to pay him back. His front lawn was some special blend of grass – too fancy for some punk to cut it. The work wasn't bad, except for not getting paid, and I only cut the lawn twice because the guy didn't want me doing any more work. He had probably decided he didn't want me anywhere near his precious car ever again.

During summer vacation, Coby and I ran away from home nearly every week to the woods in back. We outfitted our little red wagons by making cubbies from duct tape and cardboard to stow away our camping essentials. Our run-away-carts were loaded with snacks, matches, pocketknives, and all the other stuff we needed for a day. Each wagon had a quiver of arrows tied to one side and our cheap bows hanging on the other. We never actually ran away from home, but we needed to get away and escape for an afternoon.

We were playing erotic games in the underbrush. A small fire was burning under a rusty smoke stack, from the old pot fort, we had found in the woods. We heard an animal rustling in the bushes nearby. Soon, we realized it wasn't a stray cat or a raccoon. It was a person. Whoever it was had walked along the Bisset Drain from the end of the block. We heard the noise coming towards us, slinking along the scrubby tree line. They said something and the tone of the voice gave him away. It was Snock.

Coby said, “Leave us the hell alone, Snock!”

“Yeah, Snock. Get out of here you fucking weirdo!”

Maybe it was our fine cursing, maybe we were simply catching up in size and he couldn’t take advantage of us anymore. He had probably found easier prey. I don’t know why he left, but he did. He left us alone and he never tampered with us again.

But because of the things he had done to us and what he had shown us we learned about sexual pleasure before we knew what it meant or how to handle it.

Snock and Billy Garner were, I think, about the same age. It’s hard to tell because Snock was always getting held back at school. Bill and I were often in the same woods where Bentley got to us. Billy could have, but never did, take advantage of me the way Snock had. The only weird thing Bill and I did was sneak out of his camper trailer one night to spy on his sister. *His own sister.*

She was getting dressed after her shower as we hid in the shadows in the front lawn. Bill swore to me she wouldn’t be able to see us. He said the lights inside would reflect off the windowpane and create a mirror effect inside her room. But she did see us, and when she did, she screamed, “What the hell are you doing out there, Billy? You little creep!”

In the morning Mr. Garner asked him, “Why the hell were you peeping on your own sister?”

I did a similar thing about a year later. I walked into Wren and Contessa’s bedroom after Wren had gotten out of the shower. She sat there naked on the edge of the bed, knees tucked up to her chest trying to cover herself but not covering anything at all. Wren looked at me with sadness and contempt in her eyes and said, "Get the hell out of here, right now, Stephen Mark!"

The following summer, Billy and I were riding bikes on the trail to the fairgrounds. We went there with plans to break into some of the buildings. After coming off the dirt trail by the horse track we rode through the grass parking lot. The grass was knee high and full of weeds. The lot would be cut down to stubble soon because the county fair was less than a month away. Everyone was looking forward to the upcoming fair.

Pushing our bikes, we strolled through the empty midway past the Lions Club hamburger stand. During fair week, I loved grabbing a burger, fries, and a Coke and sitting under the flip-up awning on a spinning barstool. There was no way we could get into the Lions Club. Those old farts kept the place sealed up tight all year long.

We walked to the next building by the grandstands. The restrooms. There's another one by the fairground entrance. Small cinder block buildings divided into his and her privies. During fair week, the toilets were maintained by black men and women from out of town. I always got the impression they were husband and wife teams. They came for fair week, sat in the johns all day long, cleaned, filled supplies, and handed paper towel to you when you finished washing your mitts. They would say, "Hello," broadly smile, and say, "Yes, sir," and, "Yes, ma'am," and wait for you to throw a tip into their cigar box. They earned every bit of that money because they gave our *white asses someplace clean to make our stink.* Other than one black girl in town adopted by a white family, those custodians were the only black people I saw growing up in Huron County. God bless 'em.

Someone had kicked open the restroom doors, ripped off the hardware, and left a useless lock dangling from the door. Probably the boys who built the pot fort. We walked into the men's room and pissed in the dry urinals. After shaking it off (don't shake it more than three times or you're jerking off) we went to the grandstands to see if we could get in.

The grandstand door facing the horse track was always bolted from the inside with a steel rod deep in the concrete. No good. Bill and I tried a door on the side of the building, but it had the same steel bolt as the one by the track. We didn't try the door on the opposite side because we assumed it was locked up like the first two. But there was one more door we could try, the main entrance at the rear of the grandstands which went through the concessions to the bleachers.

We carefully inspected the door. This door's frame and lock arrangement were different than the others. It would be easy to force open. Bill pulled out and unfolded his lock knife, placed the blade between the two doors, and slid it up and down. Wiggling the tool, he felt resistance when it touched the bolt. He pinched the bolt with the blade and jiggled the knife handle.

"I'm going to push on the door. When I say so, you reach in and undo the lock. You got it, Stevie?"

"Yeah, I got it."

"Okay now, be careful."

He pressed the door. The wood frame groaned and the aluminum sheathing buckled as the door twisted. Bill gave the word, I reached in, pushed the bolt, the door squealed and it opened.

"Aha! We're in!"

"Cool."

We walked around looking at the empty concession stands. Everything was covered in thick dust. There wasn't much in this area but we noticed a door leading underneath the bleachers. There was no lock. We walked into the long triangle shaped corridor and found rodeo barrels, brooms, framing lumber, long pieces of common board, and sheets of plywood. There were folding chairs, raincoats, aprons, and baseball caps. Then we saw something interesting – an entire roll of admission tickets. We each peeled off a long section, folded the tickets into neat packets, and put them in our back pockets.

Before leaving, we checked to see that nothing looked out of place, locked the door, left the window lock unlatched to get back in later, and climbed out the window.

Bill stopped and said, "Be casual, act like were supposed to be here, like were doing maintenance or picking up trash."

We walked our bikes across the empty grounds, through the woods, and back to my house. We talked about the free tickets along the way. We could use them for the tractor pull, the rodeo, or the demolition derby. Shit, if we wanted to, we could go to every event at the grandstands this year. This year's fair was going to be amazing, just fucking amazing.

Later that week, I went back to the fairgrounds. There was nobody on the midway, in the barns, or on the racetrack. I climbed through the window we had left unlocked. I made three trips. Each time, I balanced a few long boards from under the bleachers on my shoulders and took them home. The first trip went well. After the second run, my mouth was dry. Needed a tall glass of ice water or iced tea, but I couldn't stop now, I had to make a third run for more lumber. I needed five more of the long boards to finish my new tree fort. With the first two loads, I picked up the boards and carried them loose on my shoulders. But on the third and heaviest load, I tied the wood with bailing twine.

On that third run, I tripped and fell to the ground. I burst out crying from the sudden jolt of pain running though my elbow and shoulder. I rested for a few minutes and continued. Made it through the trail by concentrating on my breathing. Passing air in through my nose. Out through my mouth. Counting breaths as I trodded along the path. Imagining I was Simon of Cyrene carrying the Cross for Jesus. I made it through the woods. Made it to my back yard. Made it to my tree and dropped the last load of lumber on the ground.

In the middle of fair week, Bill and I met up on the midway. Grinning from ear to ear, we waited in line for a *free* tractor pull. We handed our tickets to the man at the gate. He looked at our tickets, paused for a second, looked at them again, and said, "I'm sorry guys, these tickets aren't any good today. They must be from an event earlier in the week. I can't let you in." He returned the tickets to us.

"That's a bummer."

"Yeah, what a bummer."

"Hey, where did you boys get those tickets? Did you buy them today?"

Billy said, "We found them lying on the ground and figured we'd use them for the tractor pull. Why let them go to waste?"

The man looked at us with raised eyebrows. We backed away, pushed past everybody in line, left the area, and walked as fast as we could into the crowded midway.

I liked spending the night at Bill's house. Sometimes, we crashed out on sleeping bags in the house and fought over who got the comfy couch. The Garners parked their camper trailer under a couple of apples trees. We preferred sleeping out there.

One summer night we stayed up late talking about our collections, fishing, and keeping aquarium fish. The conversation turned to talk about girls and Bill asked if I had a girlfriend.

"Well, yeah, I got a girlfriend, but you probably don't know her." There was no girlfriend, I'd never had one.

I asked Billy if he had a girl and he said he was in love with Kiki. Her old man was an attorney. He owned a huge cottage on Saginaw Bay. He blabbed on about how beautiful, smart, and rich she was. *Yeah right! Dream on Billy!*

The night passed by, dawn was on the eastern horizon, the sky was fading from deep dark blue to dusky pink streaked with shades of light blue. We had stayed up all night bullshitting. Crinkling the cellophane bag, Bill grabbed a handful of pretzels. After eating a few, he realized how stale they were and shoved the pretzels into a half empty cup of Coca-Cola. It fizzed, bubbled over, and spilled onto the Formica countertop.

"We need to catch some shut eye, Stevie. We'll get some breakfast in a couple hours when we wake up."

Sleep settled in. It swept over me like a wall of rain clearing dust from the fields in a summer thunderstorm. I slept for a couple of hours without dreaming. I woke up knowing I needed more sleep. The trailer swayed and rocked as we got out of our bunks. We stretched, yawned, and walked to the house.

Inside the kitchen, I sat at a round table penned in by a matching refrigerator and an upright deep freeze. Billy was getting some dry cereal. The Rice Krispies tinkled in the ceramic bowl as I poured the cold milk. We sat there and ate.

After a long silence, Bill started talking about his crush. *Not Kiki again.* I was still sleepy as hell and I couldn't take it. *He and his fucking Kiki.* His chitter-chatter about her was never going to stop. It was too much!

Something was building inside my head. A deep pressure I'd never felt before. A gnawing sensation behind my eyes. My head felt like a pot of water simmering. Percolating. Bubbles rising and coming to a boil. After a few minutes of his babbling, I couldn't take his bullshit anymore. I exploded from the chair, flailing my arms and hands, and bounced up and down at the edge of the table.

"There's no fucking way a country boy like you could date or, dream-on, marry someone like Kiki. She's used to having the good things in life. Guys like you never get girls like her. That kind of shit only happens in movies." I called him an asshole and stormed out of the house.

Grabbing your bike, you ran down the driveway. Trying to get on the bike, you stumbled and kicked up some gravel. You pulled yourself together, climbed on the bike, and pushed your feet onto the pedals. Pedaling as hard as you could, panting and pumping, you drove your legs using all your strength, all the way to your house. You tossed the bike onto the front lawn and you fell down with a thud into the dewy grass. Lying on your back, you stared up into the pale blue sky. You lay there looking for discernible shapes in the clouds while trying to catch your breath. How long were you there? A few minutes? An hour? You don't know.

Five

At one of my cousin's weddings, I was outside hiding in the Cordoba. Which cousin? I don't remember. You wouldn't remember either if you had almost a hundred first cousins. I also don't remember because my dad's family *and my mom's family* were invited to this wedding.

There I was, working the steering wheel, playing with the knobs and controls, driving down a road in my imagination, when Mom knocked on the window.

"Stephen, you're going to suffocate in there."

"The window's cracked, Mom. I'm not going to suffocate."

"We're going to Our Lady of Lake Huron so we don't have to go to church in the morning. You want to go with us? Or you can go with Uncle Bob to help with chores."

"Why do we have to go to church again? We already went today."

"The wedding ceremony is a special Mass for the bride and groom. It's their Holy Sacrament with God. It doesn't count for us."

"Oh, *whatever.* I'll go with Bobby then."

"Okay, that's fine."

My favorite uncle pulled up in his blue Ford LTD. It looked like a family car, but under the hood lurked a predatory cat purring, stretching, and ready to pounce. I got into the car. Bob turned on the radio and tuned in CKLW. Pulling out of the parking lot, he drove down the street a few blocks and turned right. We passed St. Mary's Church in Parisville, where the wedding took place, passed a row of small houses, a run-down country store, and a questionable bar. With one hand on the wheel, he looked over at me, smiled, and stomped on the gas. The accelerating force pressed my back and shoulders against the seat. We cruised along at a solid clip. The speedometer needle was buried, and stayed buried, all the way to the stop sign at the corner by Halfway Tavern. Many of my aunts and uncles enjoyed drinking beer there after softball games.

Looking side-to-side, Uncle Bob said, "You've got to watch for the State Bulls here. It's a speed trap." He looked back and forth a second time. I nodded my head in agreement and repeated to myself, *Got to look out for the State Bulls.*

He tore off from a dead stop and left black marks on the pavement. Driving like a speed demon we made it to Section Line Road in no time at all. Bob rolled up to the intersection, slowed down, looked both ways without stopping, and turned right. The car pointed straight down the road as he cruised above the center line.

My uncle taught me to drive a tractor a couple of years earlier.

He was plowing snow in the driveway while I sat on the wide fender above the huge rear wheel. When he finished clearing the snow, he stopped the machine and killed the ignition.

"Want to give it a try, Steve?"

"Do you mean it?"

He nodded his head.

"Heck yeah, I want to try it!"

He sat me on the cold metal seat, stood behind me, and leaned on the tractor's fender. "Your feet barely reach the pedals, but I think you'll be all right." He explained how a tractor has a clutch like a motorcycle or snowmobile, showed me the throttle lever and how to set your speed. "That pedal there is the clutch and those two are the rear brakes, one for the left wheel and one for the right. I'll connect them for you."

I turned the ignition key, set the throttle low, and slowly let up on the clutch. I couldn't handle the pressure from the clutch and lost my foothold on the pedal. The front end made a wheelie as the transmission slipped into gear. With one hand on the wheel, the other trying to reduce the throttle, timing perfectly fucked, my right hand bounced up and *raised* the throttle. The motor roared. The force of the racing engine lifted the front of the tractor even higher – it seemed to stay in the air forever – and then it came crashing down as I slammed the double pedaled brakes. It hit the ground with a loud thud, the engine sputtered, stalled, and a puff of sooty black smoke burped from under the exhaust cap.

Bob aimed the big blue car down the road and gave the 8-cylinder everything it got, opening all four barrels and flooding the cylinders with gasoline. The engine bellowed and roared as we floated down the road. Half a mile from the farmstead Bob let off the gas and coasted the rest of the way. The engine purred quietly as we rolled into the crunchy, potholed, cement driveway.

"Let's go do them chores."

Later that summer, a bunch of us from church had a smorgasbord picnic at the park. We had set up a good spread in the pavilion between the library and the playground. On the other side of the park, behind the see-saws and swing sets, is the town's pickle factory. You could always smell the sour brine vinegar in the park. On a hot day, with the right breeze, the stench wafted through the whole town. It was nauseating. The stink lingered for decades after the factory was closed and bull dozed to the ground.

Hanging out at the pavilion, I was sitting on the back of the banana seat, rolling back and forth on my bike. The burgers and dogs were almost ready. The older kids were talking.

"What's he doing?"

"Who?"

"That kid on the bike."

They looked as a gangly teenager sped across the lawn on his beat-up bike. He drove into a big tree, car-omed off its trunk, bounced off another tree, and drove straight into a clump of overgrown juniper bushes.

I said, "That's Bentley Snock."

We watched as Snock plowed through the dense junipers and came out the other side of the hedge. He crossed the driveway, smashed through another cluster of shrubs on the other side of the tarmac, and rode to the bell pole. He threw his bike down, pushed a few kids out of the way, and cut in at the front of the line. Some kid had just reached the top and rang the bell as Snock yelled up to him, "Hurry up, kid!"

"Who is he?"

"A boy from school. He used to be in my grade but

he got held back a couple of times. He's some kind of pervert. A real creepy kid."

"What's a pre-vert?"

"He's a person who forces other people to do things they don't want to do. A sick person who needs help."

"Oh."

"But you don't have to worry about him, Stevie. Stay away from that weird Snock kid and you'll be all right."

But it was already too late. It was too damn late. Too damn late for Wren, Coby, Stosh, myself, *and a bunch of other boys in my neighborhood.*

The enuresis pad on my bed was no longer working. I was passing more water than before, soaking half the bed. A bed which I now shared with my little brother. Sometimes, Jake would wake me before I realized what had happened because he was already lying in my piss. Mom decided something had to be done. She stripped the mattress, scrubbed it, and allowed it to dry in the sun. "Sunlight's the best disinfectant." Mom slid a plastic cover over the dry mattress and zipped it shut. She placed a fresh absorbent pad on top of the hermetically sealed mattress and then made the bed.

When my brother and I climbed into bed that night the new bedding squeaked as we shifted around trying to get comfortable.

"I feel like were sleeping on a giant diaper."

"It's okay. We'll get used to it."

"Yeah, I guess you're right."
"Goodnight, Steve."
"Goodnight, Jake."

My favorite cousin, Rodney Zajac, lived near Detroit. He grew up in the suburbs and I grew up in a small town of around 3000 people. But Bad Axe is an incorporated city, so technically we were both *city boys.*

My parents and Rodney's parents had left the farm for good when they grew up and got married. Mom pursued nursing, and Dad worked in meat cutting and retail management jobs. Rodney's mom, Aunt Lily, became a hairdresser, and his dad, Uncle Marcus, worked in a Ford assembly plant in Detroit.

Lily, the last-born child, right after my dad, was a stunning looking woman. She dressed fashionably, liked to wear high heels, and always had perfectly styled hair. On a bad hair day, she wore a wig to cover up the bird's nest. She was a thoroughly modern woman.

Uncle Marcus complemented his beautiful wife with his tall, dark, and handsome looks. He wore light colored suits, flashy ties, white patent leather shoes, a smooth white belt, and he smoked long white cigarettes.

Marc and Lily were a well matched, sophisticated Polish couple. They were beautiful people, they knew it, and everyone in our family knew it. Aunt Lily and Aunt Nina are Dad's sisters, and Uncle Rusty and Uncle Marc are first cousins. I know what you're thinking, believe me, I know.

I felt like a city boy even with my small-town-country-boy streak. Despite my parents' farming background, and how much I loved being on the farm, I knew I was better than my other cousins who grew up on the farm. I'm sure Rodney probably felt this way too because he enjoyed visiting his grandma Zajac's farm in Kinde but loved living in the big city.

At weddings and other family gatherings, Rodney and I chased our *inferior* cousins, and they, in turn, would chase after us. We liked to hide, come bursting out from our hiding spot, and run after them. We teased them, shouted verbal insults, and made childish personal jabs. "You're all a bunch of farm boys. God-damned shit-kickers." And they returned the insults. "You're a couple of city slickers. You goddamned townies." But Rodney and thought it was funny, because we were city boys, and our taunting probably didn't bother our cousins, because, well, they were farm boys.

Uncle Marcus didn't think it was funny. He yelled at us on one occasion. *He was pissed*. "Why don't you quit fighting with each other for Christ's sake? You're cousins."

After he scolded us, we went inside to use the can. When I came out of the bathroom I ordered a Coke. Rodney already had a drink, but it didn't look like a pop.

"What are you drinking?"

"A beer."

"How the hell did you get that?"

"I took it off a table." He set down his empty cup.

"You're kidding me. How?"

"It's easy. I'll show you in a minute." He waited until an older couple got up from their seats to Polka. Bussing their table, he picked up some Chinette plates and two beers. He walked to the kitchen, dumped the trash, carried the two beers back, and handed one of them to me. The drinks were completely untouched.

"That was too easy."

"I know it."

He raised his glass, I tipped mine to his, and we said, "Cheers."

We sipped our barley pops. The taste was not appealing. We drank the brews quickly, hoping nobody would notice, or care, that we were drinking beer.

"Are you done yet?"

I said, "Yep," and handed him the empty cup. Rodney gathered up some more discarded plates and two more beers. The old farts smiled and nodded at him as he cleared the table. Were they on to us or merely being thankful? After throwing out the trash, Rodney came back with the beers.

"Nice work, cous', really nice work."

"After these we should get a couple more."

"Good idea."

"Yeah, but this time you get them. You saw me do it. Walk up and start clearing the table."

"Okay, okay. I'll do it."

I finagled two more beers by doing what he had done and then we drank them as fast as we could. Soon afterwards, things got a little weird. I think we were what you would call intoxicated. Plain old dumb drunk.

Rodney and I went outside to run around the reception hall. We ran faster than humanly possible. Found our shit-kicking-farm-boy cousins and chased them around the building. Round and round, we ran ourselves to exhaustion in pursuit of our god-awful cousins. When we stopped, Rodney and I were panting and drooling, completely out of breath.

We sat down in some folding chairs at the edge of the parking lot, trying to catch our breath, and looking at cute girls from *the other side of the wedding.* As we scanned the scene, checking out the ladies, Rodney noticed two lonely drinks sitting on a picnic table. I knew exactly what he was thinking. We walked over and picked up the beverages. They were mixed drinks. He said his was a 7 & 7 and the one I had was a whiskey sour. My drink tasted like a strange tropical punch with a sour lemony kick.

"I want to try that one."

The 7 & 7 tasted dank, dark, and complex with a little bit of citrus flavor but it wasn't as good as the whiskey sour. Either one was better than plain old beer. The cocktails were delicious.

I had drunk beer before, taking sips from my dad's bottle, Grandpa Booms's, or one of my uncle's. They often offered me a taste. It was like pouring beer into a dog's bowl. It might be funny to watch, but what's the point? A dog doesn't know what the hell it's doing. The poor animal's depending on you, he trusts you to care for him, but they gave *this poor little puppy* sips of beer anyway.

Alcohol wasn't part of my family's daily life. Mom and Dad weren't big drinkers. But beer, wine, and booze always flowed freely at family events and parties with friends. So, it's not surprising that when I was ten, maybe eleven years old, I started getting shit-faced drunk with my cousin Rodney at family weddings. When Rodney wasn't at a reception, I drank by myself, but it wasn't much fun drinking alone. Our parents never seemed to catch on to what we were doing.

When our cousin Melissa, Nina and Rusty's daughter, got engaged, Rodney and I knew her wedding would be a complete blowout. Her fiancé, Muzey Polskie, was a talented musician and could play almost any instrument. He was going to play in his own band at the wedding reception. Muzey would definitely play his accordion. How can you perform a Polka without an accordion? And would probably play his clarinet too.

I was geeked about the big day. All of Melissa's bridesmaids were total knock-outs. My little sister Tessa was going to be the flower girl. With her beautiful light blonde hair, she fit right in with my attractive cousin and her bridesmaids.

I found out over four decades later that Contessa was not looking forward to being flower girl that day. She didn't see why the family was so excited about her having to wear a dress, curl her hair, and kiss a boy – the ring bearer. Disgusting!

The wedding party was going to be fun for the whole family, except me, because I had caught mononucleosis. Everyone kept telling me mono is the kissing disease. How embarrassing. I hadn't kissed anyone before, well, I had, but does kissing a boy count? I hadn't kissed a girl and kissing a girl was what I wanted to do.

I didn't go to the wedding ceremony that afternoon because I felt so crappy. Fever had wiped me out and I was too ill. Mom and Dad came by the house after church to see how I was doing. Feeling a bit better, I decided to go to the reception. We packed into the Cordoba and headed to the hall in Pigeon.

I felt good when we arrived, but Mom and Dad left the car unlocked in case I needed to rest later in the afternoon. We went inside and put our jackets and Mom's purse in a dusty coat room. I sat by myself at a long table, waiting for Rodney, looking around to see who else was there.

All the bridesmaids were skinny, had long legs, slender arms, and perfect champagne tits. The wedding was in early fall, the trees were changing color to deep red, yellow, and burnt orange. The girls standing up, dressed in shades of russet, brown, and gold, coordinated well with autumn's palette. They looked stunning and I couldn't keep my wandering eyes off them. They must've have noticed me ogling them. I knew what it felt like to get unwanted attention.

Weeks before the big wedding, Mom bought new outfits for Wren, Jake, and I to be as well dressed as Contessa. Mom bought me a brown suit and I started wearing it to church instead of my lavender jean pants, lavender jean jacket, and my favorite blue floral shirt.

One Sunday before church, I was letting off some steam, riding my bike at the end of South Street near the ball diamonds. Some girls from school shouted cat calls and whistled at me. Cruising by in my Sunday best, I felt a raging blush, embarrassment, confusion, and shame from their unwelcome stares. They were *checking me out,* and I liked it, yet didn't like it at the same time.

At the reception, I kept looking for Rodney. I hadn't seen him in a long time and was looking forward to seeing my cousin. After a while, I couldn't sit straight or keep my head level on my shoulders. I felt like shit again and went outside to lie down in the car.

About an hour later, Rodney found me curled up in the back seat. I was half awake, groggy, and my crazy fever had returned.

Earlier that week, my temperature rose quite high and I had walked in my sleep. I'd never sleepwalked before. A weird thing happened on my slumbering walk. I had appeared like a wraith in the kitchen and was reaching for something in the cupboard.

In the living room Mom looked up from watching TV and said, "What are you doing with the pepper?"

"I need it."

"But why do you need the pepper, Steve?"

"So, I can measure my ear."

Mom got up and took my temp. It was a hundred and three. She gave me two aspirins and kissed my hot brow. "I love you, Stephen Mark. Now go back to bed so you can get some sleep."

Dad got out of his recliner and gave me a big bear hug and a scratchy kiss from his scruffy face. "I love you. Get your little *dupa* in bed. I hope you feel better in the morning."

To this day, I don't remember the pepper shaker incident at all.

I wasn't near that level of heat at the wedding reception because I do remember talking with Rodney. That is to say, I remember exchanging words with him. What words? I don't know. But after we talked, thank God, he went inside to find my mom.

She came out to the car with Dad. Taking a thermometer from her purse, she shook the mercury down in the glass tube. I automatically opened my mouth, she placed it under my tongue, and I clamped down.

"His fever spiked, Buck. He looks kind of *peaked.*"

"How bad is it, dear?"

"Almost as high as *the other night.*"

"Oh, boy. We'll have to pack things up and go home."

"We can't do that, Bucka. Contessa's the flower girl today, she's having the time of her life. I'll call Mom and see if she can sit with him."

She walked to a nearby pay phone, inserted two thin dimes into the slot, and rolled the numbers on the rotary dial. Slip, clip-clip-clip-clip-clack. Slip, clip-clip-clack. Grandma Booms answered the phone. They spoke for only a few seconds because Mom had interrupted another conversation and couldn't tie up the party line.

Mom drove me halfway across the county to Grandma's house in Harbor Beach. Mom and Grandma must have talked for several minutes, but I was somewhere else lost inside my head and don't remember much about the visit. All I remember was Grandma putting me down in one of her squeaky iron beds upstairs. She tucked me in, I pulled the warm, musty quilt up to my nose, fell asleep, and woke up, the next evening, at home, in my own bed.

From first to sixth grade, the Catholic kids in Bad Axe went to catechism during public school hours. The church pulled us out of class on Released Time and took us to Sacred Heart School while the *other* kids had an extra recess or worked on art projects. Once a week, every week, the whole school year, they bussed us across town to learn the teachings of the Roman Catholic Church.

Most of the boys had used the restroom before loading up, I however, distracted by a piece of floating dust, or adventure in my imagination, walked straight to the bus. After rolling down the road a few minutes I noticed an intense pressure in my bladder and realized I had made a mistake.

I could have imagined an endless sandy desert, but instead saw myself standing in front of the toilet. A pristine white bowl waiting for me. I stood over the basin, looking down at the cool water. But I wasn't standing in front a toilet – I was on a bus full of noisy kids. The pressure was too much and I couldn't clamp down on my bladder. I tried crossing and uncrossing my legs but it was no use. I let loose and the flood came. A dull, wet warmth spread from a small spot on my left pocket to a large patch covering the upper thighs of both pant legs. I took off my hooded sweater and tied it around my waist.

All the kids got off the bus and went inside for catechism.

A few minutes into the lesson I raised my hand and

asked the teacher, “May I go to the bathroom, please?”

“You should have gone before class, Stephen.”

“I didn’t have to go then. Can I please go now?”

I got up and left the room before she could answer. I passed Father Carroll Eoch going up the stairs to his office as I went downstairs.

The heavy wooden bathroom door swooshed open and its hinges squeaked as it slowly shut. My footsteps echoed off the concrete floor in the stillness of the small room. I grabbed a few feet of paper towel and took it to a stall. I daubed at the wet spot on my pants, took off my soaked underwear, rolled them in paper towel, and stuffed them into my jacket sleeve. I tied the jacket around my waist and carefully adjusted it to conceal the dark spot on my jeans.

I went back to class and sat without talking for the rest of the hour. I watched the slow hands of the clock – they weren’t even moving – waiting for it to be over so I could go home. After what seemed an eternity, we were dismissed.

Briefly stepping onto the bus, I told the driver I was walking downtown to meet Dad at work. I had walked home from catechism before and the driver didn’t think anything of it.

I walked past the church to the end of the block, crossed Huron Avenue, walked past the courthouse and jail, turned onto South Street and went straight home.

Downstairs, I removed my soiled clothes, washed myself, and threw the dirty clothes onto the laundry pile. I put on a fresh pair of underwear, clean jeans, and went upstairs to make myself a snack.

An inquisitive old broad was watching me as I smelled the scented candles at Dibble's. This kind of stuff, especially incense, had recently become a thing for me. It probably had something to do with Mom's new hobby.

I looked up and saw Dion Wise, a kid from school, browsing in housewares. He saw me looking at the incense and other crap but he walked over to say hi anyway. We became friends in third grade. Doodling on our homework papers in the back row of math class. While everyone else finished their work, we made sketches of the cartoon characters from our textbooks.

He said, "What are you doing here? I'm here with my mom."

"With my mom too. I'm trying out all the incense flavors. She burns it when she's belly dancing."

"Really? Your mom belly dances?"

"Well, yeah."

Mom had taken up belly dancing to workout, get toned, and maybe to entertain Dad. Her new exercise routine required some gear. For authenticity, she bought an Arabesque LP album, harem outfit with bangles and bells, a snazzy bra top, and burned incense in the house despite hating the stuff. She got terrible headaches from the strong frankincense when our priest burned it in church. He walked up and down the center aisle to bless everybody with thick smoke oozing from his swinging incense burner. She couldn't stand it!

I said, "These smell great when Mom burns them."

"They smell good even if you don't light them. Ever try the incense cones?"

"No, but they're the same as sticks, aren't they? Mom puts the sticks in the planter. Right in the dirt."

"You could do that with cones, but most people use one of these brass burners, or even better, one of these cool Buddhas."

"That would be the best."

We bought a red one and a black one, each statuette was flecked with touches of gold paint. Bought some red cherry incense cones, strawberry ones died pink, and we split the packages in half.

After checking in with our moms, we rode our bikes to my house. We went downstairs to sit on the old couch.

"Do you want the red Buddha or the black one?"

"Black. Definitely black."

"Okay, I'll take the red one. You want something to drink? We've got sun tea."

"Yeah. I love iced tea."

I went upstairs for the drinks. The glass bottles were still warm from brewing on the patio. I placed several ice cubes into tall Tupperware cups and filled them with tea. We drank two quarts while trying the new incense burners and filling the whole basement with fragrant smoke. The incense smelled nothing like the real thing, lit or unlit, but we didn't care.

Mom got home from the store and came downstairs fanning the smoke away from her face. She told us that she had a good chat with Dion's mom, Grace. Our moms had talked it over and decided I could go to Dion's house anytime. Dion's family lived on a small dairy farm a half mile past the Bad Axe city limit.

"We should go right now, if that's okay with you, Mrs. Kubacki."

"That's a great idea. Mom, can I?"

Mom agreed, but said I needed to be home by six o'clock to clean up for supper.

We biked to Dion's house riding on the shoulder of M-53. We went past the seedy, tiny-ass apartments which you could rent for a month, a week, or just for the day. We rode past the dilapidated trailer park, the used car lot, and the local country and pop rock radio station, WLEW. When we pedaled past the junk yard, I saw a field full of cows and knew we were at Wise Dairy. It was right across the road from the drive-in theater.

We walked inside his house, a sweet double wide trailer, said hi to his mom, and talked for a few minutes. She told Dion to go next door and introduce me to his grandma and grandpa.

Inside the old farmhouse, Grandma Wise brought out a tin of vanilla cream cookies and a pitcher of iced tea. We sat down at the kitchen table with the old farts and watched a black and white TV set with rabbit ears.

Dion told me how they made tea. They steeped the tea in hot water with twice the amount of tea bags needed, added a ton of ice, and then it was ready to drink.

We sat sipping the tea. It was delicious.

His mom walked in and joined us in the cramped kitchen.

"Steve should probably be going home soon, Dion. The Kubackis eat at six like we do. He's got to be home before the six o'clock whistle."

When my *busia* and *dziadzo* sold their farm and moved into Bad Axe, Aloysius gave one of his sons an early inheritance – the house, the barn, the land – and wrote him out of their will. Soon afterwards, Uncle Junior sold the place to a real estate developer.

There was a lot of gossip about the real estate agent who bought their farm and dozens of others in the area. Rumors spread about his plans to build a new golf course and subdivisions filled with cookie cutter gingerbread houses, but the land developer sold it all to Detroit Edison. They had plans to build a nuclear power plant which would ruin the natural beauty of Verona Hills.

The county had already changed the farmland when they diverted a section of Willow Creek, reversed its flow, connected it to Rock Falls Creek running to Harbor Beach, and made Willow Creek's headwater flow, *unnaturally, in two opposite directions.*

Edison said electrical demand had changed and didn't build the powerplant. Many people feel that local political pressure was the real reason they declared it a surplus property and sold the land to the Michigan Department of Natural Resources.

Grandpa Kubacki's house, his brother's farm, and all the other farms within nine square miles were turned into hunting land. The houses and barns were bulldozed and buried in the foundations of the old basements. All that's left are the driveways and grass parking lots where the yards used to be. The DNR rented out some of the acreage to sharecroppers and let everything else go wild. Nothing is on the land where the Kubacki farm once stood. It's merely the dirt that built the hills and the creek that tries to wash them down as it winds its way through the valley into the Verona swamp. I hope it stays that way forever.

When Grandma and Grandpa Kubacki left the farm, they bought a cute house in Bad Axe. A fixer upper that needed fresh coats of paint, new siding, and some roof repairs. Needing help around the house, they asked me to mow the lawn, and Wren and Contessa to clean the house.

After putting the mower and gas can away, I went inside. Grandma was waiting at the door. With a broad smile on her round face, she handed some cash to me and my sisters. I took it from her and counted it.

We all said, "Thank you, Grandma."

Holy crap! I couldn't believe how much she had paid me, and she gave Contessa and Wren a lot of money for their work too.

Mom and Dad were sitting across from Grandpa at the Formica kitchen table. I sat down with them. A pull-down ceiling lamp shed dim yellow light onto the table. Grandma pulled the light down closer and sat with us. Grandpa was silent, sitting there with his head bobbing. He looked exhausted.

I didn't know it then, but he would be in a nursing home within a couple of years. That's where he faded from the hulk of a man, we all knew, into a living skeleton, disoriented and alone.

I was at the old folks' home when the family told him the bad news as he lay there staring at the ceiling, barely moving. I'm not sure he knew who was visiting him. But a dull look of recognition came to his face when we told him his Lucy had passed on. He died eight months after *Busia* died.

At the dimly lit table, Grandpa looked at me and said, "I hear you're collecting coins. Do you have any paper money in your collection?"

"No. Why?"

Billy Garner had shown me his silver certificates, and we liked looking at pictures of large denomination bills in coin books, but I didn't have any collectible currency.

Grandpa slowly pivoted in his chair and pulled out his wallet.

"Well, because you might be interested in this."

He shuffled through the tattered leather thing and removed a neatly folded-up bill. After gently unfolding it, he set it on the table. It was a two-dollar bill with a red seal. It looked really old. I wondered if this bill had been inside his Mason jar in the hollow tree back on the farm.

Next to Thomas Jefferson's face, the date said 1928 – on back, Jefferson's neoclassical house, Monticello. The backside of a modern two-dollar bill shows The Committee of Five presenting The Declaration of Independence to John Hancock for his approval. The fine cloth fibers inside the paper were barely holding the bill together. Deep creases formed a cross on Jefferson's boyish face, with a small t-shaped hole in the center.

"This is yours now."

I took the rolled-up cash from cutting the lawn out of my front pocket, smoothed it flat, set the old two-dollar bill on top of the lawn money, and I asked Grandma if I could have an envelope.

It was the summer after sixth grade when Grandpa gave me that two-dollar bill. I was almost in junior high and still wet the bed. I avoided drinking liquids before bedtime but it never helped. The pads and plastic sheets saved some clean-up for Mom, but they didn't stop me from wetting the bed. My parents suggested a new plan.

"If we wake you up during the night to go piddle, maybe that would help."

Dad always went to bed after watching the eleven o'clock news. He'd come in to check on us kids and started waking me up at eleven thirty for a piss. Sometimes, when he came to check on us, I had already wet the bed.

Dad would say, "Oh, Steve, not again," and he'd get Mom out of bed to clean up the mess.

When Mom woke me before dawn for a pee the bed was usually dry and I didn't have to go. Mom gave a kiss to Jacob and me, tucked in our blankets, and we fell back asleep. Then I would fall into a dream where I'm standing in front of the bowl, my shins touching the cool porcelain. Everything was vivid and seemed so real. I let the stream go and I'd wake up in a pool of urine again.

I was still pissing the bed at night in junior high school when I got a paper route with my friend, Thomas Argent. It was my first formal job. The deal was sealed by our good word and handshakes with Mr. Chapman. We collected money from our Detroit Free Press customers, created a fund to pay for the papers, and knew our expected pay for the month. We received some kind of tax document, which I gave to Mom, but Argent probably filled his out by himself. Tom and I would meet at the end of each month to pay the boss.

The customers wedged collection envelopes into a door jamb, placed them under the doormat, or crammed them in a crack behind their mailbox like the money didn't matter. I found envelopes on top of shrubs and laying on front lawns. They didn't give a shit about the money and I didn't give a shit about it either.

At first, I tried to set aside money to square-up with Chapman. But no matter how hard I tried, I would spend it on video games at the arcade, doughnuts, and junk food. *The money burned a hole in my pocket.*

I just couldn't save the money. I started taking customers' envelopes, pulling out the green, and stuffing it into my pocket with no intention of setting it aside. I figured the uncashed checks, payable to Detroit Free Press, would cover the bill to Chapman. Why not pay myself first? I spent the cash and never had enough checks to cover my half of the bill.

When meeting up with Chapman I made any lame ass excuse, like a kid who had lost his homework, to buy a day or two, and said I'd get the money for him as soon as possible.

I could cut Grandma Kubacki's lawn or clean her house. But why bother? My fail-safe way out was asking my parents for money. They gave it to me every time I asked. Every single time.

My paper route was supposed to be a learning experience, but I didn't learn anything about handling money or running a business. The only thing I did learn was how to wake before dawn, get out of bed, and go to work. At least that's something, isn't it?

On those early mornings I sprang up like a soldier rising from his bunk in the barracks. I went outside, grabbed my bike, and rode to Tom's house in the cool early morning air. On Argent's front porch, I inserted ad flyers and coupons into the papers. After loading my shoulder bag with papers, I got on my bike and was gone.

A good customer of ours had a fridge full of pop in their garage. *Everyone should have a pop fridge.* They told Thomas and I to help ourselves. Of course, they meant anytime we were delivering their morning paper, but I would stop by and grab a Pepsi when it was my day off. When it was my day to make deliveries, I grabbed two pops, one to drink on my route, and one for afterward.

When I finished the route, I biked to Murphy's. With a light breeze the bakery filled the downtown area in a smarmy, sugary fog. I liked to buy a chocolate frosted, custard filled Long John and a raspberry filled jelly doughnut whenever I had cash. Then I cruised home munching on my sugary breakfast.

Around this time, Dad hired a carpenter, if you want to call him that, to build a wall around our basement toilet and shower. The guy did such a shitty job my old man had to hire another guy to finish it. The first guy had built a half-assed wall but my parents couldn't stand the idea of scrapping the work he'd done. The second guy, a master carpenter, made the hack's mess as plumb, square, and level as he could with several blows from a sledgehammer.

It wasn't a proper wall because the first guy did such bad work. He had built the wall with a one-foot gap along the top. The clown didn't know how to frame the wall up to the ceiling joists. The second contractor not only repaired the shoddy work, but also installed deep storage cupboards in the bathroom, and running along the stairs built a coat closet and boot closet with sliding doors.

I started taking naps on the old couch on the outside of the new bathroom wall. After a while, I was sleeping down there at night. I draped an old purple duvet from the basement foundation wall to the bathroom wall. Put all my clothes in the coat closet and my tennis shoes in the boot closet. Dragged my dresser and all my other crap into the basement. *I finally had a room of my own, and finally had some damn privacy.*

Dad and I eventually built a wall to replace the fancy duvet. I repurposed the duvet by stapling it to the ceiling joists and snapped an upside-down lampshade over the bare bulb in the ceiling. We also installed a door from Grandma Kubacki's house, scrapped out when she remodeled her bathroom.

One of Dad's friends asked him if we would be installing a fire exit to replace the small steel framed basement window in my room. "Nah, Steve's smart enough to run up the stairs or climb out through the window if there's a fire."

The old man was satisfied with the work, but I

wasn't. My bedroom needed one more thing to make it mine. I removed Grandma's old doorknob and replaced it with a keyed lock.

In junior high everyone changed into shorts or sweatpants for gym class. The girls' locker room had individual shower stalls for each girl, but all the boys piled into one huge, dull yellow, ceramic tile shower. Our Phys Ed teacher at Bad Axe Junior High was in there while we undressed, showered, and changed back into our regular clothes for class.

I needed a backpack and didn't have anything to wear except crappy hand me down shorts from who knows where or old sweatpants from Mom. I wanted to buy a BAJHS t-shirt and shorts from the store at school. I was always in the office buying pens, pencils, and eraser ends, but didn't have enough cash to buy the outfit. *That money's going to burn a hole in your pocket.*

My parents wouldn't buy a backpack for me. They thought it was a waste of money. But after some pestering Mom agreed to buy the outfit. After she bought the blue shorts and shirt, I carried it to school in an old paper sack. I used the bag for about a week and then replaced it when it wore out.

One day after school, I was eating a snack, watching *The Match Game* on the tube, and doing math homework. *Steve's mom never bought chips or candy. He usually made a snack out of blank.* There wasn't too much homework, I did most of it at school and usually didn't bring any home. The drudgery at school was easy for me. But not for my friend, Coby, who often asked me to help him do his homework. We'd go to his house, I'd show him how to do the work, and we'd eat *his mom's delicious snacks.*

After finishing my homework, I put it away in my Trapper Keeper and looked for my brown bag. I didn't see it anywhere. *Where the hell had I left the damn thing?* I looked by the back stairs and in my bedroom downstairs.

"Mom, have you seen my school bag?"

"That crinkled up grocery sack?"

"Yeah. Remember? You guys wouldn't buy me a backpack. You said it was a waste of good money."

Rooting around in the furnace room Mom had accidently burned the old grocery bag and used it to light a fire. She thought my bag was trash and threw it into the furnace without looking inside the old sack.

As the woman explained what happened, you realized she had burned your gym clothes. You could feel the shape of your face changing, contorting, and twisting. You stopped listening to her words. The sounds she made mixed with the rumbles and whines of the furnace. The blower fan kicked on with a roar and started pushing amazingly hot, dry air into the house. Her lips were moving but no sound was coming from her mouth. You went to your room, slammed the door, and locked it.

One fine day, Dion and I were hanging out at Tom's

house. There wasn't anything good to eat in Argent's kitchen. We wanted to buy some junk food but didn't have any money. Someone suggested we borrow money from Rudd's giant Heineken bank full of change. We knew he would never miss it. He had hundreds of dollars in the beer bottle bank. Luke had been feeding change into that plastic bottle for years.

He had an afternoon paper route at the Huron Daily Tribune, was decent with his spending, always had money in his wallet, and whenever he bought something, he threw the change into that larger-than-life beer bottle.

Dion, Tom, and I walked to his place and entered the small mudroom on the side of the house. Standing on the narrow landing we breathed in heady musks and skanky white florals – lily, jasmine, and tuberose – from stored products, boxes and boxes of it. Mrs. Rudd had the stuff stacked up and down the stairs and on every other flat surface in the house. Avon cosmetics, candles, and perfume everywhere. The house door was locked. We looked at each other and shrugged our shoulders because it was usually unlocked. I suggested we try Luke's bedroom window.

We walked to his window and got inside the overgrown shrubs against the house. Dion and I popped the aluminum screen. I told Tom and Dion to weave their hands together and I stepped on their hands to reach into the bedroom. My belly was pressed against the window jamb as I reached in, grabbed the bottle, and handed the jar to Dion.

I climbed down from the windowsill.

Tipping the giant bottle upside down, we expected

a removable plug on the bottom, but it was solid plastic. We couldn't cut a hole in the bottom, Luke would notice that, and besides, the plastic was too hard to cut with a pocketknife. Instead, we carefully sliced the coin slot on top to make it a little bit wider and a little bit longer. Dion and I tipped the bottle and rattled half dollars, quarters, nickels and dimes from it as Tom gathered the coins in his outstretched shirt.

They hoisted me up again and I put the bank back in its spot. We reinstalled the window screen and ran away giggling. At the party store, we bought junk food and got all sugared up on pop, candy bars, and chips with our *borrowed* money.

Monday morning, we met at Luke's house before school. He asked if we knew anything about money missing from his bank. He had noticed the enlarged slot. We fessed up and told him we would pay him back, because, well, *we had only borrowed it.*

A few days later, Mr. Rudd saw the damaged screen while doing yard work and Luke got in trouble. To make things right with his old man he told him who had damaged the screen. What else could he do? We already pilfered his money without asking. Why should he take the heat for the damage?

Every year a spaghetti dinner was held to raise money for the eighth-grade trip to Toronto. It seemed like the whole town showed up at the elementary school for a plate of mediocre pasta, watery red sauce, and toasted Wonder Bread sprinkled with garlic salt and Kraft Parmesan Cheese. Mr. and Mrs. Rudd were going and wanted to speak to Dion, Tom, and me at the dinner.

Dion, Tom, and I met in the hall outside the gymnasium.

Long tables and benches had been folded down from the walls, like Murphy beds, to convert the gymnasium into a cafeteria. A huge line of hungry folks had formed outside the gym and trailed down the corridor, past one corner, and then around another corner of the square-shaped building. It was common for a line to form all the way around the perimeter of the school. As diners left, the eighth-graders swooped in, removed plates, cups, flatware, carried them off to the kitchen, and wiped the table with a towel drenched in bleach water.

The Rudds were eating their plates of pasta. The three of us said hello and they greeted us with silent nods. Luke couldn't look us in the eye. After a few hard looks from his folks, and a funny, face-tilting look from Luke's sister, Mr. Rudd spoke.

"You boys know why we asked you to come here?"

"Yes, we do."

"Because we're in trouble for damaging your screen."

"We can fix it for you, Mr. Rudd."

Mrs. Rudd said, "We don't want you to fix anything."

"No. We don't want you boys to repair the screen. I've already made the repairs myself."

"Then, why did you ask us to come here?"

"What do you want us to do?"

I stood in silence.

"We want a formal apology."

"From each of you," said Mrs. Rudd.

"Right here. While we finish our spaghetti."

"In front of everyone?"

"Yes. Right now."

Mrs. Rudd nodded in agreement.

We stood there stunned like a deer caught in a poacher's spotlight.

Thomas apologized first. He said why he was apologizing – breaking in, the bank, the screen – how badly he felt about his actions, and that he was filled with remorse.

"I'm sorry Mr. and Mrs. Rudd."

And I apologized too.

We waited with our heads lowered while they finished eating.

Instead of the eighth-graders cleaning up the mess, the Rudds made us remove their plates and wipe off the table. They had done something few people had ever done in my life. They punished our mischievous behavior, our criminal activity, but they didn't call our parents or call the police. They used public humiliation and our own guilt to teach a lesson. They put us in the public square, locked us in pillories, and threw tomato sauce and pasta in our faces.

I don't know what Dion or Tom got from it. The lesson I learned was that stealing wasn't wrong, but stealing from a friend was definitely wrong. Even when you were borrowing something without asking, your buddy will find out, his parents will find out, someone will find out, and there will be trouble. I already had enough trouble in my life.

Six

After snowmobiling one frigid afternoon, Coby parked the machine between the house and Dad's tool shed. We went inside to make hot chocolate. We warmed up sipping our cocoas and watched TV. Bored with the complete lack of entertainment, I turned off the set.

"What did you do that for?"

"There's nothing good on, besides there's something you got to see." I wanted to show Coby *the book.*

Mom taught the rhythm method to a bunch of ladies she knew at work and church. It was a fertility awareness class for more successful conception. Even with my inadequate knowledge of human anatomy I knew why most of them timed their periods. The women who met at our kitchen table were trying to avoid getting pregnant. They studied a book filled with yellow, green, and red rectangles arranged in grids. It was a calendar.

I had wanted to see what it was about and went looking for it. I found it on the bookshelf in the living room next to another interesting book. It was a book on human sexuality. *The book.* The book I was going to show to Coby.

We opened the book and looked inside. We had seen a lot of this stuff before. Had looked at plenty of girlie magazines and some triple-x ones too. Zee's dad had stacks of them in his bedroom closet. We knew about titties and boners and pussies and fucking. What else was there to know?

I knew this stuff well enough to have sketched detailed drawings of human genitalia back in grade school. I folded them up and put them in an old

Brownie camera. Took them out now and then to show my buddies. Mom found my camera one day. She opened the film compartment and found my sketches.

"Who drew these for you, Stephen Mark?"

"I drew them, Mom."

I don't remember what she said, the surprised look on her face is all I remember. I'm not sure if she said anything at all. She crumpled up the sketches and threw them in the trash. *She threw away my erotic art.* But I drew better pictures of titties and boners and pussies and I was a lot more careful where I hid them after that.

Mom's book had lots of things Coby and I had seen before, but there was also stuff we didn't know about yet. We were reading a section about *alternative lifestyles* when Coby said an italicized term out loud. He laughed because it sounded funny and I laughed because he had pronounced it incorrectly. He misread the word *homosexual* and said *bomosexual.* In his defense, the italicized *h* did look an awful lot like a *b,* and he had probably never heard the word homosexual before.

Around the same time, I had discovered self-pleasure and started masturbating, but had never made it to ejaculation. I didn't know what it was. I knew about penetration and fucking but didn't know about the immense pleasure of orgasm and didn't understand my own *plumbing* at all. From what I'd been taught by my parents I thought men inseminated women by rubbing their testicles against a woman's labia. They told me it was like the birds and the bees and the flowers and the trees. Which meant that human sex organs worked like the pistil and stamen in a flower. A man's testicles *pollinated* a woman's vulva. Hell, as young kids, we weren't taught proper anatomical names. Jake and I had a pee-pee, and our sisters had a *ciuściuś*. We were taught a real solid sex education. I actually believed sperm brushed off the balls and attached to the pussy lips like pollen in a flower.

I read the whole book that evening before falling asleep. It turns out that men don't pollinate women like a flower does. And after reading the book, I figured out that I wasn't gay. *I wanted to be with girls.* What were Coby and I doing? It seemed like homosexuality to me. Did that mean we were gay? But now I knew I was heterosexual, because deep down I wanted to date girls, not fool around with boys.

Recently, I had noticed some thick fluid in my ass and now I knew what it was. Coby may not have known what was happening, just that it felt good, or maybe he did know he was ejaculating inside me, but I sure as hell didn't. But now *I knew* one of my oldest friends, someone I trusted, was cumming in my ass, and I wasn't sure how I felt about it. I lay in my bed wrapped in confusion and anger, fed by envy and a disintegration of trust for Coby not telling me about it.

I had to know what an orgasm felt like and that night I found out. I masturbated faster than ever before. I went over the edge, something released deep in the pit of my belly, and my testicles spasmed.

Blood spurted out my penis and splashed onto my belly. Intense pleasure was suddenly overtaken by fear. I was bleeding out in my bed. There was a lot of blood, enough that I knew I could bleed to death. I jumped out of the bed, ran to the bathroom, and turned on the light to see how badly I was bleeding. I looked down at my belly and didn't see a single drop of blood.

I saw something else. It looked like iridescent liquid soap and smelled like bleach and hot metal. *It was my semen.* I wiped up the splooge with a wad of toilet paper. After I cleaned up, I looked into the mirror and grinned at myself. Now I knew what it felt like. I went to my room, crawled into bed, and fell into a deep sleep.

My buddy Luke delivered papers for the Huron Daily Tribune long before Tom and I delivered morning papers for the Free Press. Luke was good at it, a real businessman – *low overhead, high profit.* After school he biked directly to the printing press dock to pick up his papers. He knocked on customer's doors when subscription fees were due and asked for payment instead of waiting for envelopes to appear like Tom and I did. He kept a ledger and paid his boss, in full, on time. The kid played by the rules and always had money. He kept a few twenty-dollar bills in his wallet, with several singles underneath so it looked like all twenties, to impress everyone. He told us, "Girls dig a guy with cash." Besides always having money, he saved it in the bank and earned interest. I didn't even know how interest worked. But he was only a kid, and like any kid, he had to let off some steam once in a while.

Dion and I were riding bikes at the edge of town in a new apartment complex. Using the parking lot speed bumps as ramps, we got up speed, hit the bumps, and with some effort, we were airborne. While riding in the lot we saw a new kid from school, Rizzo Hendricks, loitering outside the laundry room smoking a cigarette. He saw us, threw his cig into the flowerbed, and walked toward us.

"Hey Kubacki, hey Dion, what are you guys doing here?"

"Jumping over speed bumps. They make great ramps."

I said, "Yeah man, it's cool. You should try it."

"It looks kind of lame to me." But he walked to his place, grabbed his bike, and joined us anyway.

We rode to the next parking lot and saw Rudd's bike leaning against a small tree. We went up to the building and waited until Luke came outside.

"Hey, Hendricks. Hey, guys."

"Hey Rudd. I ran into these guys popping wheelies in the parking lot. You want to fuck around with us?"

"Yeah, sure, but I got to finish my route first. I only have a few buildings left. You guys should help me, I'd finish quicker."

Dion said, "All right, we'll help you."

"Yeah, man," I said. "We can help."

"All right, Rudd, let's get it over with."

"Make sure each paper gets a coupon and a detergent sample."

Rizzo said, "What the fuck?"

"It's a new laundry soap they're promoting. You have to put a coupon and a detergent sample in each paper." Luke told us which hallways and apartments to hit and gave us the papers, a stack of coupons, and handfuls of samples. We split up and delivered the last of his newspapers.

After finishing, Hendricks, Dion, and I found where Luke was and threw our bikes on the ground next to his. The pile of chrome and painted steel glimmered in the bright sun. We went inside to cool off in the hallway. Luke came running down from the upper hall and bounded down the stairs.

"We're done fuckers!" He reached into his shoulder bag, grabbed some packets, starting squirting detergent, and covered us with slimy blue soap. We ran out of the building and he chased after us swinging his newspaper bag with one arm and spewing detergent with the other. Trying to get away from him, we ran across someone's patio, crisscrossed over the lawn, and ran into the next building.

Luke followed us.

We had only a moment to get ready, but the three of us took samples we had left and prepared to fight. Dion and I ducked under the stairs. Rizzo waited by an apartment, tucked in next to a door. Luke came in and we let him have it. He had samples ready and rallied against us. We made a huge mess in the corridor. The lavender scented soap was smeared everywhere on the walls and carpet.

Some of Rudd's customers complained about the mess to the paper. Rudd's manager at The Tribune asked if he had seen anybody stealing samples. They weren't suspicious of Luke and didn't ask if he had anything to do with the vandalism. The paper thought some kids from the apartment complex had made the mess. Nothing happened, we didn't get in trouble, but we didn't fuck around on Rudd's route again. There were too many nosy people around and we were damn lucky we didn't get caught.

Later that summer, Mom and Dad rented a cottage on Lake Huron for a week. Mom said Wren and I were old enough to have friends stay with us during vacation. I invited Dion.

It was a house on the beach between Port Austin and Caseville, near McGraw Park and Port Crescent State Park. There was once a town named Port Crescent, it's now a ghost town. All that's left is the iron bridge crossing the old channel of the Pinnebog, out of place landscaping plants, still arranged in rows after many decades, and the base of an old sawmill chimney.

The sawmill was built to increase production of lumber after The Great Fire of 1871. The mill harvested the charred remains of dead trees, salvaged the good wood inside the trunks, and sold the lumber to rebuild the county. The fire helped make Huron County one of the most productive agricultural counties in the State of Michigan because fire had cleared the land and fertilized the soil with ash. The new farmland created a need for better drainage and farmers started straightening and rerouting local brooks, creeks, and streams.

The Pinnebog River – from an alteration of the Ojibwa word, *binébag,* which means partridge berry – was no exception to the *tampering* of streams. Port Crescent had built two dams to harness the river's power. One wet spring, one of the dams backed up from the deluge of snow melt and heavy rain. The Pinnebog escaped its streambed and found a way to the lake by a new channel. The old channel is still there under the iron bridge but it no longer reaches Lake Huron and has created a stagnant, elongated pond which is now a popular fishing spot.

Dion snagged a big cat one day. Out in a rowboat we had dropped double-hook rigs to target perch. His rig must have been lying at the bottom and the catfish swam into it. The damn thing snagged onto the hook above its eyeball. My mom took a picture of us holding up the catch of the week, two geeky boys wearing black *Death Before Disco* t-shirts, with that fucking cat in a collapsible fish basket. The fish was almost two feet long. But it wasn't a legal hook set, besides we didn't know how to clean it, and we let that bitch go.

We spent hours in the water fishing and swimming. Dion could swim – I could barely dog paddle. When attempting freestyle, I flailed my arms, kicked my legs, and inched forward while gulping mouthfuls of water. My best trick was *swimming* in the shallow water by walking with my hands on the sandy bottom.

To kill time, we explored the area. The coolest thing in the area was the Big Rock. We got badly sunburned by spending so much time in the water and on top of that rock. Silver dollar sized blisters popped up on my back and Mom said I would probably get skin cancer someday because of overexposure to the sun.

Despite her warning, we sat on the Big Rock, without sunscreen, swimming around it, under it, and through it. The rock was covered with graffiti, etched in with a knives and beach pebbles. So, we scratched our names on it too, but scratching our names on the rock wasn't good enough for me.

Dion and I stole a can of spray paint from the cottage landlord's garage to write something big and bold on the rock. I decided to make a declaration of love for my crush at school. I climbed onto a flat sloping rock, a ramp coming out of the water, and painted large block letters declaring my feelings for my girl.

C A P T
H I G H
L O V E S
T I T S

I had earned the pothead nickname long before I smoked dope. Maybe my friends had noticed one of my hangovers after a night of partying at a Polish wedding. But more likely, they had noticed my eyes, my wild staring eyes. The name gave me aspirations for the future and in high school I embraced the name when I actually became a stoner.

A lot of boys called Daphne Buchner *Tits.* An inappropriate yet accurate epithet for a cute girl with big jugs. She and a friend had gone sunbathing at McGraw Park later that summer, walked down the beach to Loosemore Point, and saw my graffiti on the sloping rock. How could they miss it? It was larger than life. That fall at school she asked me about it.

"I saw your graffiti on the Big Rock. I know you're *Captain High*, but who's *Tits?*"

I blushed and told her, "Well, it's you, Daphne."

All week long, Dion and I roamed between our cottage, the Rock, McGraw, Port Crescent, and a nearby party store on the other side of M-25. The family that owned the store also ran a campground in the woods out back. Each summer it was filled with tents, pop-up campers, and motor homes. Every day, we went to the store at least once, some days two or three times. We spent all our money at their convenience store and were running on pure sugar. An attractive older girl, a cashier at the store, talked to us whenever we came in. She said we were cute.

"Are you two brothers? You two look a lot alike and you dress the same." We told her no. "Are you sure you're not brothers?"

"We're sure."

I said, "Yeah, we would know, wouldn't we?"

"You guys are going to be heartbreakers in a couple of years."

Hearing that from a hot chick embarrassed me, and walking out the door, I felt a boner growing in my swimming trunks.

At night before falling asleep, Dion and I talked about girls. The ones we had seen on the beach, the cashier at the store, and girls at school. We talked about sex and what it would feel like. What kind of girl do you want to fuck? Who is your favorite actress on TV? Your favorite centerfold? Do you want to get married? Raise a family? We babbled on and on.

Dion said, "How far have you been with a girl?"

"Absolutely nowhere. Not even a kiss. Just playing footsie on the couch with one of Wren's cute friends when she slept over at our house."

"I've been to second base." And I thought, *What does that even mean?*

Our talk led to the topic of masturbation. We were sure no one had gone blind, or grew hair on their palms, because both of us had tried it. Dion said he had jerked off plenty of times yet had never made himself cum. He wanted to save the first time for when he was with a girl.

"Ya gotta try it, man. It feels awesome."

Both of us were getting sleepy and we finally settled down. The cassette in the boom box came to its end and shut off with a click. A small table lamp cast dim amber light on the bare plywood walls as we dozed off to sleep.

A while later I woke with the urge to piss. *Thank God I woke up for once in my life.* I sat up and looked over at Dion in his bed. He was lying on his back, still awake. He looked over at me, holding up the sheet with one hand making a tent, and his other hand pumping up and down. He speeded up, suddenly stopped, and pulled back the covers. With a grimace on his face, he looked down at the chartreuse fluid oozing from his dick.

"I did it, man. I made myself cum!"

"Holy crap! I can't believe you did that."

He grabbed a box of tissue from the nightstand and cleaned himself up. "You were right. It felt awesome."

"I told you so."

Every evening that week we built a small bonfire on the beach. We sat around the fire cuddling, Dion with Wren, and me with my sister's friend, Leigh, and stared into the flames. Four young bodies raging with a torrent of hormones being drawn into the fire. How does a fire entice you and lure you in? And why, when you watch the fire, does it make you want to look deeper into the flames? The four of us looked deeper and deeper without knowing how to answer a question we didn't think to ask.

I thought my sister was taking one for the team, but years later, she told me she was okay cuddling with Dion. Wren and Leigh both had crushes on Dion, and Leigh had been sitting on my lap and nuzzling my face even though she didn't dig me at all. *She* was taking one for the team. *What the hell?*

When staring into a fire, it feels like you're looking into infinity. Like the illusion of two mirrors face-to-face. Have you ever held a small mirror in front of a bigger mirror? If you tilt the hand mirror at the proper angle you can look at the infinite. You can count the reflections for a while but soon you're lost in the endless number of mirror frames. Your attention fails, the angle shifts, the illusion is lost. But the glimpse into infinity stays with you, etched into your mind.

The image of infinite mirrors opens your imagination and helps you understand the physical reality of an infinite universe. The vastness of the physical universe, its infinite depth, is more profound than an optical illusion. My mind couldn't comprehend the endlessness of the universe. Thoughts of it kept me awake at night. Thinking about it is like staring into the face of death. Infinity is eternal and death is eternal. The end of life is like the end of the universe, they both stretch on and on, forever. Or do they?

In my large family it seemed as if someone was

always dying. Sometimes death came suddenly. Sometimes it came slowly and gave the dying person time to leave on their own terms, and the living, time to accept it. Growing up, I had seen lots of death, and wasn't afraid of death, dying, or physical pain. What I was afraid of is not knowing what's beyond this life. Not knowing if the stories about heaven were real or fairy tales. Not knowing if salvation through Jesus was real or a bunch of bullshit. Does believing His teachings give you eternal life? *I didn't believe a carpenter from Nazareth was my only chance for salvation.* Why did I need Jesus to get into heaven? Was His path the only way through the life-gate or were there other paths up the mountain? Did everyone get in? Everyone is born, everyone lives, and everyone dies. Why wouldn't *everyone* go to heaven regardless of what they believed?

Maybe, there was no path at all. Perhaps, when we die, we're dead body and spirit, *and there's nothing at all.* A void.

If there was a heaven, I didn't care what it looked like. It didn't matter if there were angels sitting on clouds playing harps, that God had a long white beard, or my lost loved ones greeted me with open arms. My deepest concern about heaven was what would I do for all of eternity? These are ideas that kept me awake at night and filled my day with anxiety. One day all these thoughts stopped.

I enjoyed streaking and running around nude in the woods behind my house. One August day during fair week, I had stripped and piled my clothes near the sledding hill. I ran from the hill down the trail that runs alongside the ditch to an open field behind my house, turned around, and ran back to the sledding hill to get dressed.

The silence of the afternoon suddenly broke. A shot had fired from somewhere behind the houses on my street. The gun shot seemed to come from Mike Braeburn's place. There was a short pause and the gun fired five more times. I ducked into the brush behind a small spoil tip and fell to the ground as the bullets rippled through the air above me.

Silence.

It's probably a fucking pistol and they're reloading it now. They're going to start shooting again. I was lying on the ground and couldn't move. A volley of six more shots bursts through the woods.

Someone yelled, "Is somebody back there?"

You couldn't answer them. You're naked, they'll hear you and know who you are. What if you die there and you're found like that? You have to get the fuck out of here.

A new hobby shop had opened in Bad Axe. They sold model cars, airplane kits, paints, and not much of anything else. They had zero backstock in the warehouse and put the empty space to use by filling it with pinball machines and video games. On warm days, the owners kept the storeroom door open to let in the breeze.

The open door stared at Argent's front porch. Tom and my other buddies could look from the porch through the bank drive-through into the back door. The arcade was in clear sight, looking at us, teasing us, and telling us to come spend our money. Drop a coin into a slot for the cheap thrill of flashing lights, ringing bells, and the tinkling of metal on glass. Drop a quarter and battle Space Invaders or shoot up a field of space rocks on Asteroids. I started spending a ton of my money inside that wonderful place.

The coins disappeared and my pocket was empty when I left. When my money was gone, I needed more to keep playing. I started selling wheat pennies and Indian head pennies from my coin collection to get cash. The buffalo head nickels and Mercury dimes went next. Then I sold half dollars, silver dollars, and even the red seal two-dollar bill Grandpa Kubacki gave me. I sold my entire coin collection to play fucking arcade games.

After a long afternoon in the arcade, my friends and I were at Argent's house and wound up spending the night. We stayed up late hanging out on the front porch. Argent's large house invited you with its smiling stoop. The stair railings, built like walls, were at least sixteen inches wide. Tom and I were sitting on top of the bulky rails with our feet dangling over the edge. The others were lying on the cool cement floor or swaying back and forth on a graceful porch swing. It was one of the hottest nights of the summer, still balmy at two in the morning. Tom was now on his back, lying on a wide rail, staring up at the American flag flapping above him.

He suddenly got up and removed the flagpole from its bracket. I watched Tommy, expecting him to remove the flag from the pole, fold it into a neat triangle, and take it inside the house. Instead, he started walking down the sidewalk with the pole propped on his hip as the banner floated in the air. Tom was singing the notes of a Sousa tune as he marched.

We got up, followed him down the sidewalk, and stood at the edge of the street to watch his procession. He did not make a legal stop at the intersection. Thomas turned left, marched down the center of the Port Crescent Avenue and headed north to the end of the block. He made an about-face at the intersection, rotating from north to south, marched back, and saluted us as he passed by. We didn't move from our spots as he approached the flashing red light at the main intersection in town. He spun around under the stop light, marched down the center lane to his block, stopped in front of us, and took a bow. Tommy burst out laughing, we roared along with him, and all of us ran down the sidewalk to his house.

Thoroughly exhausted, we went inside and fell asleep on the couch, two armchairs, and the fuzzy carpeted floor.

A few hours later I woke to a familiar thud – a stack of heavy newspapers dropping on the front porch. I looked over and saw Tom was already awake. He laced up his shoes, stood up, and stretched. Removing his shoulder bag from the hook, he went out to the porch and loaded papers into the bag. Tommy got on his bike and rode away.

If I had been a more thoughtful friend I would have gone with Tommy to help him out. Instead, I stretched out on the couch and went back to sleep. About an hour later, I woke to Mr. Argent shaking my shoulders.

"Is Thomas awake? Did he go out to deliver the

papers?"

"He took off a few minutes ago, Izzy. I'm not sure when. I fell back asleep as soon as he left."

Izzy said, "Mr. Chapman has been getting calls from customers who haven't received their papers."

"I'll go see if I can find him and help him finish the route. We stayed up late last night. He's probably really tired this morning."

"Okay Steve, that sounds like a good idea."

Dorjzaly said, "I'll go with you."

Tobias Dorjzaly was a stand-up guy and was always willing to lend a hand. Tobi and I went out to look for Argent. We rode along the usual route. As we went along, we found the papers were already delivered. Dorjzaly and I split up and within ten minutes he found Tommy sleeping on a customer's front lawn. As he walked to the house, the owner came outside and saw Tom lying in the grass. Tobi helped Argent get up from the lawn and they explained to the man why he had fallen asleep in his yard.

The three of us finished the paper route. Afterward, we put our money together, I only had some pocket change, Tommy and Tobi coughed up most of it, and bought a dozen doughnuts from Murphy's Bakery. We took the doughnuts back to Argent's house and woke the other guys. As we sat eating our sugary breakfast, I decided it was finally time to stop going to the arcade and stop spending so much money. It was embarrassing not having money to pay my share and I should start saving to buy that new Atari game console too. I simply couldn't live without it.

Argent and I lived a few blocks from each other.

He was spending a lot of time at my house ever since his mom passed away. Sometimes, he came with us to family events. At a cousin's graduation party, Tommy was accused of stealing a twenty-dollar bill from my uncle's wallet. I knew he didn't take it because I had.

When my aunt asked about the missing money, I said, "Tommy would never steal. He's not that kind of person. There's lots of people here. Anyone could have taken it."

One afternoon he went with us to Grandma Booms's house for Sunday dinner. My uncles, Bobby and Kenny, had recently bought a three-wheeler ATV. One of those things that they stopped making because they realized how dangerous they were. They could roll over so fucking easy. My uncles used it to herd cows, run back and forth between their three farms, and for the sheer joy of speed. The week they bought it Bob took me for a ride and showed me how it worked.

They got it one winter, and Bobby tricked me by saying he had bought a snowmobile and would take me for a ride. We walked through the snow drifted yard to the barn. I waited in anticipation as he opened the tall sliding doors. "There it is, Steve, my snowmobile!" It was the three-wheeler.

We buzzed around the driveway and into the snow-covered field, buffeting through the drifts. After a few minutes Bob stopped the machine.

"Want to give it a try, Steve?"

"Heck yeah, I want to try it!"

He got off the machine, scooted me close to the handlebars, and then climbed on the padded seat behind me.

I drove quite slow at first, but once I had a feel for it, I let her rip. As I was winding up into third gear my uncle poked me in the ribs and said, "You're going a little bit too fast."

Before the afternoon Tom came with us to Grandma's, I had been riding the three-wheeler for several months. *I was an expert driver.* I told Argent about the machine and said we should take it for a ride.

Bob and Ken had parked it inside the workshop. Tom and I went to the shed, rolled back the huge sliding door, and there it was. I climbed on and grabbed the handlebars, flicked the ignition switch and pressed the start button. To get Tommy used to it, I drove in circles around the chicken coop where Bobby used to keep his rabbits. Then I flew down the driveway, onto the shoulder of the road, up to the nearest intersection, and turned left onto a gravel road.

I probably scared the crap out of Tom when I veered off the road and barreled into a ditch. I went down one bank, hit the ditch bottom at a slight angle, and ran up the other side into the field. The tall plants were starting to tassel out. Driving along the edge of the field I looked for a break in the rows, a spot where seed had not grown. I wanted to turn around in an empty space and go back to where we came into the ditch. Unable to find a good spot to turn around, I thought, *fuck it*, rolled into the plants, made a wide U-turn, snapping the stalks and smashing them to the ground. I turned around and crashed into the plants again. Moving ahead in a straight line, I reaped the corn as stalks smacked against my shins. I made a large circle and then a second one to form a giant figure eight. After destroying hundreds of corn plants, I drove back through the ditch onto the gravel road. We cruised down the road for a minute, I stopped the trike, revved the engine, and turned it off.

"Want to give it a try?"

"I don't know, man."

"It's easy. It's a big tricycle with an engine. You should give it a try. I'll show you how." I climbed off and showed Tom where the brake and clutch were and gave him a quick run-down of how everything worked. "The accelerator is like one on a minibike. You can drive a minibike, can't you?" He slid forward. I got on the seat behind him, pointed down the road, and said, "Let's go that way."

"Okay."

Tom made a careful U-turn and then drove up the road. Dust and bits of gravel flew into our faces. Clipping along at a steady pace he followed my tracks on the road. Then he surprised me by following my tracks into the ditch. *Would he be able to worm in and out of the ditch going this fast? This is not going to be good.*

I jumped off the back of the seat as he plowed into the bottom of the ditch. The thing almost stalled when Tommy hit the embankment on the other side, but the machine jostled and continued to climb up the bank. The tires grabbed the ground and sent the machine bolting forward.

I got up on my feet, dusted off my pants, and looked out of the ditch to see Tom and the bike flying through the air. He bounced off the seat as he held on for dear life. The front wheel hit the ground, the forks turned inward, the bike rolled over and threw him over the handlebars. Argent landed on his ass, the machine landed on its wheels and kept going, it zigzagged for a few seconds, and then stalled out.

I was okay, and thank God, Tommy was okay, but holy shit! Argent almost died that day. Because of me. What the fuck?

When dad had torn down the fort he built at the back of our garden, I needed a new place to hang out. I had built a small triangular platform between three stout branches of the box elder behind the garage. The tree had lots of character, at least that's what I thought, but Dad hated the tree.

The platform wasn't enough. I needed more privacy than the tree's branches could provide, so I started putting up walls. Two walls had windows with large flip-up panels like you might see on a roadside fruit stand. The third wall had two small flip-up windows, but the panels looked more like ones on deer blind. Closed in the roof with reclaimed two-by-fours and half sheets of plywood and tar papered it to keep the rain out. I ran a fifty-foot extension cord form Dad's shed to provide electricity. It was the shabbiest tree fort I'd ever seen, but it was mine, all mine.

This tiny triangular box sat thirty feet off the ground. The rooftop was forty feet up. It was the size of a very small bathroom. When I was up there by myself or with one buddy it was fine, but with two or more friends it was crowded. The thing was too damn small. I decided to tear out the largest wall to build an addition.

When I had removed the wall, I assembled four-by-four beams from scraps of two-by-fours nailed together to make three floor joists. I spanned the beams from the existing fort to a limb eight feet away. The addition would nearly triple the square footage from twenty to fifty square feet.

I nailed scraps of common board onto the joists to create a floor. The kite shaped fort was incomplete because there were no walls or even a railing in the new section. I had used every scrap of wood from Dad's shed and garage, all the wood stolen from the fairgrounds, and had nothing left to complete the fort. My friends and I enjoyed the open deck for a couple of weeks but I had to put up two more walls, or at least a railing to make the deck safe.

My buddies helped gather lumber from wherever they could find it to finish the project. Rudd and Argent got pieces from their garages and Dion scrounged up some wood from his grandpa's barn and milk house. We installed a gently sloping roof over the new and old parts of the fort but left the nearly flat roof above the old section to make a mini loft.

An unexpected gift from Tobi showed up when his old man's truck backed down our neighbor's driveway and stopped under the tree. As we unloaded the lumber, Tobi's old man asked, "What the hell are you guys going to do in that fort? Have a circle jerk with all of you sitting around cuffing your carrot?"

The Dorjzalys had recently remodeled their basement. They had lots old boards from the demolition work – beautiful rough-cut pine, sealed with dark amber varnish. When I put up the old planks, they made the place look classy. One beautiful wall in an otherwise complete piece of shit fort.

My friends and I were admiring the varnished wall one day when Luke suggested hanging a bunch of Playboy centerfolds on it. "They would look awesome up there."

That's exactly what we did. Luke provided a lot of the posters but my other buddies pitched in nudies for the wall too. The wall of pinups was a work of art, a floor-to-ceiling installation of beautiful women in every shape, size, and color. We arranged columns of them at the top and bottom of the wall with a band of reclining nudes running through the middle. The word spread and lots of boys at school wanted to see the ladies. Lots of kids wanted to see the collection of nude posters. Wren and her friends took a look and two cute girls from school asked to see the wall. These two girls had heard about it and didn't think it was real. Dion and I showed it to them one day after school.

Frances Sawicki said, "This is amazing."

Her friend agreed, "Yeah, they're beautiful. I can't believe it."

Dion and I couldn't believe it. These young ladies liked the wall of smut my buddies and I had created. They couldn't take their eyes off of it. I could tell they loved it because the girls' eyes kept darting back and forth as they admired the nude models.

Frances came out of her daze and said, "My family's going to Poland next month. Dion's getting the mail for us while were on vacation. You guys should hang out at the house and use the pool."

"That would be great, Sawicki."

"Yeah, that's awesome. Thanks Frances."

If I wasn't up in the tree fort staring at the erotic wallpaper, or looking at girlie magazines, I was dreaming of real girls. But being clueless about girls, all I could manage in the real world was pinching girls' butts in the hallways of my junior high.

Our principle, Mr. Fairfield, tried to keep things civil when he patrolled the halls, but he couldn't be everywhere at once. When he did catch you grabbing some ass, he gave you a look, a single look, or shouted your last name, and stopped you in your tracks. He also handed out lots of after-school detentions. *The eighth hour.* Fairfield thought spending some of your free time after school might teach you a lesson.

Mrs. Fairfield liked wearing A-line dresses and always wore color coordinated high-heeled shoes. Waiting at our desks before English class, you could hear her smart shoes clicking and clacking as she walked down the hallway. Jolie Fairfield was the first person to teach me anything important about writing. She used Strunk's *The Elements of Style* and Warriner's *English Grammar and Composition* to guide us. I highly recommend them to anyone interested in upping their writing game. Mrs. Fairfield emphasized the importance of avoiding passive voice sentences, gave us strategies to avoid any form of the verb *to be,* and most important of all, she taught us how to write about *anything* using the classic five paragraph essay. I've used it ever since eighth grade – now with a lot more than five paragraphs.

One day in class, she brought out her Bible, opened

it, and before she read a single word, Tommy raised his hand. She immediately said, "Settle down, Mr. Argent. I'm reading this Bible as Literature. This has nothing to do with the separation of church and state." Tommy looked at her with his mouth hanging open.

The Fairfields didn't take any shit from any of the kids, but we got away with a lot of crap in Jean Ventdebois's classes. He conducted the seventh- and eighth-grade bands, taught music class, and history lessons in the school library. The band room sat directly below the library and he was often running up and down the fire escape between the first and second floors. Every day during music class, we sang a syllable run to warm up. It was "Doobie-doobie-doo" and we added an extra "smoke" at the end of the run much to Jean's chagrin.

In history class we sat at large rectangular tables, three students to a table. He had a hard time keeping us under control because Jean wore Coke bottle glasses and couldn't see what we were doing. The big library tables also blocked his view and concealed our activities. Another boy and I liked to crawl under our table during class to molest a girl who sat with us. We took turns poking and grabbing at her legs and crotch from under the desk. She dealt with our stupid juvenile bullshit every day. Jean would catch us every now and then. When Ventdebois asked what was going on, the poor girl covered for us and said, "Steve dropped his pencil again."

The meanest thing the kids at school did was mess with Ventdebois's baton. His conductor's baton was a fine thing crafted with a rosewood handle and a pure white shaft that must've been ivory. The ongoing gag in band class was hiding his baton somewhere in the room. We hid it under his sheet music, in a filing cabinet, or inside an instrument case. Once, we hid it in *his tenor sax case* and it was the last place he looked.

One kid liked to grind it to a point in the pencil sharpener. After the fourth or fifth sharpening, Ventdebois was going a bit crazy because the boy had ground off so much of his beloved baton. He didn't know how to deal with the abuse from his students and usually resorted to the same old thing. It was hilarious to hear him shout, "Eighth hour! Go see Fairfield!" as he pointed at the band room door and sent you to the principal's office across the hall.

The baton disappeared one day and he absolutely couldn't find it. I had hidden the thing where he would never look. A couple of girls found it before band class started. They had gone to the bathroom together, as girls often do, and as one was squatting on the bowl something fell from the ceiling. It fell right between her legs into the toilet. The girls took a closer look and knew what it was.

Before class I had sneaked into the band room, grabbed it, and climbed to the top of a storage shelf. I threw the baton into the girls' bathroom exhaust vent. When the girls found it, they fished it out, cleaned it up, and returned it to Jean as he was tuning up the band.

Mr. Ventdebois had had enough of our shit. He whirled around swinging his arms, pointing the baton at me, and shouted, "Kubacki, eighth Hour! Eighth hour! Go see Fairfield! You go see Fairfield, right now!"

"Okay, okay, I'm going!" *How the fuck did he know I did it?*

"Two eighth hours!"

My porn collection was getting too big to hide under my mattress. I decided to build a box out of pine wood and put a padlock on it. After it was built, the small box sat on the corner of my desk. I had a black and white photo pinned to the door. The picture showed an older classmate of mine. A close-up of her legs. She was wearing two-toned cowboy boots. When my parents asked what was in the box, I told them it was my hope chest.

One boring afternoon, I unlocked the box, took out a magazine, and flipped through the pages without much interest until I saw something that locked my eyes to the picture. That look. That pose. That long hair.

As I began, I heard a noise in the laundry room but it didn't make me stop. The wash machine or water softener was always making some weird noise in there. Then I heard the toilet paper tube rolling on the other side of the wall. Someone was using the john. I heard the toilet flush and then silence.

"Hey, what are you doing in there?"

"Mom? What the fuck!"

She was looking down at me as I scrambled under the blankets to hide my activity. She stepped off the toilet and went upstairs to start making supper.

The problem was the bathroom wall didn't quite reach the ceiling. If that hack carpenter had done a decent job, it wouldn't be this way. But it was never closed in properly and a twelve-inch gap ran along the top of the wall.

After Mom peeped over the wall and caught me jerking-off I closed in the gap with scraps of particle board. My repair stopped all peeping activity. My buddies were pissed because they couldn't watch Wren using the toilet anymore.

In the fall, I wore an old, dark blue vest for my eighth-grade school picture. The same vest I wore for my *fifth-grade picture.* In the photograph, my hair is tousled and greasy. You could tell I didn't give a shit about my clothes, my appearance, and probably didn't give a shit about anything at all.

We got our yearbooks every year in the spring. Not many people asked me to sign theirs, if someone did, I skipped the personalized note and only scribbled my initials. A handful of close buddies signed my yearbook, but no one else did.

I'd been avoiding him and hadn't talked to him in months, but for some reason Coby asked me to sign his eighth-grade yearbook. "Okay, I'll sign it for you." I took the book from him and wrote, *To my dear friend Coby, Why don't you fuck off and die?* then I signed and dated it.

At the end of class Mr. Coho was looking at some of his students' books, reading notes and signatures, and adding his own. All the jocks were asking him to sign their yearbooks.

Coby handed his book to Coho, “Hey coach, will you sign my yearbook too?”

“You got it, Coby.”

After he signed Coby’s yearbook, Coho was flipping through reading the notes and signatures. As he read, his cheerful expression turned sour. He handed the book back to Coby and looked at me.

“Hey Mr. Kubacki, why did you write such a nasty note in Coby’s yearbook?”

“Coby and I are old friends, Coach. It was a joke.”

“Yeah, Mr. Coho, it’s a joke. Kubacki and I are always goofing around like that.”

Seven

One day after walking home from school, I went into the kitchen and made a stack of mini sandwiches out of Saltines and creamy peanut butter. I turned on the TV to watch *The Match Game. The kid came home from school and made a snack out of blank.* After the game show was over, I got up and turned the rotary dial to watch cartoons on another channel. Satisfied with my choice, I slumped to the floor. As I watched *Tom and Jerry,* the TV screen suddenly folded in on itself and formed a funnel. The colors melted from the edges of the funnel to the center of the screen and slid down into a small midpoint of intense white light. The bright white dot disappeared and left an empty screen. A blank field of black. The fucking TV set was fried.

We had gotten a lot of rain. Grandma's lawn needed to be cut and her house needed cleaning too. Despite the heavy rainfall, the lawn was nothing but a bunch of tall weeds poking through the gray grass. I wanted to save money for a new video game. Grandma usually paid me fifteen dollars for knocking down the weeds in the yard, twenty for cleaning her house, but this time she gave me two twenties.

Maybe what my folks said was right. I had been trying to save up for months and didn't have anything to show for it. If I could only save a month's worth of earnings I would have enough to buy the Atari game console and a few cartridges. But Mom and Dad were right, I couldn't save money because, "That money's going to burn a hole in your pocket."

It didn't matter if I saved up for the game now because we didn't have a working TV. It didn't matter at all. I might as well buy more LPs and cassettes, stop in at the bakery for a doughnut, buy a pop at the party store and enjoy what I earned. I could also blow some money at the arcade since I would never be able to buy an Atari.

Dad went out and bought a new TV. My siblings and I were elated. He picked up the set downtown at Yageman Home and Auto. A tall, stretched out man who didn't talk much delivered the television. He wore striped blue coveralls and white booties over his heavy work boots. Dad helped him carry the set into the house. They hoisted it over the back porch landing, set it on the dining room floor, and I wheeled it into the living room.

Before the man had left the house, I had plugged it into the wall, attached the roof antenna wire, and connected the Pong. I turned the TV on and the screen lit up immediately. You didn't have to wait for the tubes to warm up like our old idiot box. You didn't have to rotate two separate dials to reach a UHF station. You could select channel 25 by *pushing two buttons.* No dials. This set was digital. No tubes! Holy crap! It had a remote control and the clicker didn't click it whined like a dog whistle. The weird thing is, only Wren and I could hear the high-pitched whistle.

Contessa and Wren started to play a game of Pong tennis. To make things fair, Contessa used the wide paddle and Wren used the narrow one. After playing a round, they turned off the console and found one of those corny afterschool dramas on the tube. We heard Mom outside rolling into the driveway. She came in the house and set her funny white cap and bandage scissors on the snack bar.

"What is this?"

Wren said, "Dad got us a new TV!"

"Isn't it great, Mom?"

"Buckley! Ding dang it! I told you we can't afford a TV. We talked about this. Now we'll have to eat liver and onions twice a week. We should have saved up to buy a new TV. Where did you get it? You must have bought it on credit. No Buck! The TV has to go back. We have to return it. Oh, heck."

Dad often rebelled against Mom's budget constraints like when he bought a Dairy Queen calendar with coupons attached. Mom said we couldn't afford the calendar, or the treats, even with the coupons. She stills enjoys telling this story decades after it happened.

I figured things would settle down. Mom would get over Dad's spending and we'd probably keep the new TV. Now I had a good reason to cut more lawns and save my money to buy a new Atari to replace the boring old Pong console. I did some work for Grandma Kubacki the following week.

First, I cleaned the house. Then I worked up a good sweat pushing the lawn mower. Sweat, gas, and oil mixed together and was rolling off my hot, sticky skin. I finished cutting the lawn and went into the house for a glass of Grandma's bubbly homemade punch. She mixed Hawaiian Punch with 7-Up, the stuff was amazing. Grandma sat down and drank a cup with me. She put two twenties *and a five* in my hand and look me square in the face. Her eyes sparkled like St. Lucy's on a prayer card. Lucy's beautiful eyes.

"You did a good job today."

We sat enjoying our drinks and eating a tube of Pringles. In the other room Grandpa shifted on his recliner making the vinyl upholstery cover squeak. He was sitting there staring at the black and white TV set. He didn't seem to notice us at all. Tobacco juice dribbled from his chin as he tried to spit into his milk jug. He cleared his throat. The disheveled old man shouted something at the TV and spewed droplets of brown saliva into the air.

While we enjoyed our refreshments, Grandma started talking religion. Grandma went to Mass every day. She rode with us on Saturday night and went with Rusty and Nina to church Sunday morning. During the week she rode to church with a friend, or if that couldn't be arranged, she walked several blocks to get there. I stretched my arms to the ceiling and yawned as she talked about the Bible.

You tried going into that small space inside your head. Smiling a dim idiot smile, you went there for a few seconds. Usually, you could go there for as long as you wanted, but you snapped out of the trance when the old woman said something that caught your attention. She was saying something about tearing apart your own body.

"If part of your body causes you trouble, cut it off. It is better to live without it." Grandma smiled and looked at me. Her bright blue eyes shimmered.

"Okay, Grandma, I've got to go now."

I wadded up the money, put it in my pocket, and walked outside. As I climbed onto my bike, I couldn't help wondering what the hell was she talking about. What was the old woman trying to tell me? I didn't understand. I didn't understand at all.

The fair had come to town. It showed up every year in the second week of August. The carnival started with a Western rodeo on Sunday and always ended Saturday night with the demolition derby. My family went to the rodeo almost every year. We weren't horse people, but we liked to see Mr. Braeburn riding on his horse, Little Mike. The carnival trucks, campers, and horse trailers started showing up late Saturday night and kept rolling in until Sunday morning. All kinds of people came to town during fair week. They parked their cars bumper-to-bumper on South Street. *They knew about my trail.*

On that hot Sunday night, I had gone to bed early. Unable to sleep, I was lying in bed for an hour or two with nervous energy gripping my imagination. Lying there staring at the ceiling, I saw a small light shining through the bedroom window. I blinked my eyes as the light bounced along the ceiling. The flashlight turned off and came on again.

Someone whispered outside the open window. "Hey Kubacki."

What the hell?

I got out of bed.

"Who's out there?"

"It's me, Raphael Dorjzaly, and Tobias is here too."

"Hey Steve."

"What are you guys doing here?"

"Tobi and I snuck out of Grandma's house. We're

going to the fairgrounds to watch the carnies setting up rides. You want to go?"

Tobi and his brother Raphael always stayed at their grandma's during fair week. They saved up their money for the fair but never seemed to spend any of it except on food and sometimes a game or two inside the arcade tent.

I removed the steel framed window, pushed out the wooden screen, and crawled onto the wet grass.

Tobi said, "Do you know the trail to the fairgrounds?"

"Of course I do. Let's go."

We went to the fair and watched the carnies set up rides. It wasn't magic after all. A lot of tough looking, hard-working men, and a few tough-as-shit women, put the rides together. We walked around for a couple of hours watching them park huge tractor trailer generators, laying down miles of electric cable, assembling carnival rides, and then we went home.

When Raff and Tobi crept back into their grandma's house the old woman might have been enjoying a cup of chamomile tea before bed and heard the boys. Or maybe they were lousy sneaks and she heard them from her bedroom. I don't know how she busted them, but they got in trouble, and the trouble reached me on Monday morning.

Mom and Dad were pissed. They made me sleep in my old bedroom with Jake. *My old bedroom.* On Tuesday I made an apology. I told them what they wanted to hear, anything to sleep in my own room again. I told my parents it was Tobi and Raff's idea and that I had *never even thought of sneaking out before.*

I wanted my room back, and within two nights, I got what I wanted. But Mom and Dad did sit me down for a talk. They had had enough of my bullshit. The shenanigans at school – poor Mr. Ventdebois and Mr. Fairfield – you're getting too many eighth hours. How many eighth hours can you get? There are days when you're there for a ninth or tenth hour. With all the eighth hours, you're spending more time at school than at home.

Mom finished by saying, "We're sending you to the Teen Ranch. We've had enough of your conniving."

"You can't make me go there. I'll run away from home before you could take me. If you manage to get me there, they won't be able to keep me. I'll go live in the woods." I ran down the basement steps in three bounds, went into my room, slammed the door, and locked it.

Later that week, after things settled down, Dad and I went to one of my uncle's farms to look at his new grain dryer and storage elevator. As we approached the farm he didn't slow down and turn into the driveway but drove by and continued down the road toward Rapson. He drove another mile, turned left onto the dirt road, and rolled into a parking lot in front of a modest house.

We were at St. Joseph's Church.

"What are we doing here?"

"Steve, your mother and I figured since you won't go to the Teen Ranch, or talk to any head shrinkers, maybe talking to Father Benjamin would straighten you out."

"I'm not going in there."

"Oh, Steve."

Dad got out and walked around to my side of the car. I locked the door. He glared at me, turned around, walked to the steps, climbed the porch, and knocked on the door. A priest dressed in black opened the door and let Dad into the house. Several minutes later they came out of the rectory and walked to the car. I opened the window to hear what they had to say.

"How are you today, son? I'm Father Benjamin."

"I'm not your damn son."

"Oh, *Jezus kocha mnie!*"

"Hmm. I see. Yes, yes. Maybe, we can go inside and have a talk. Would that be okay with you, Stephen?"

"No."

"Stephen Mark!"

"You can't make me go in there, Dad. You can't make me fucking go in there."

The old man gasped, the priest shook his head, and both men stood outside the car glaring at me. The priest whispered into Dad's ear and they went back inside the parish office.

I waited for a long time before Dad came back to the car. He wasn't frowning but he wasn't smiling either. Reaching to the driver's side, I lifted the latch to unlock his door. He sat behind the steering wheel and stared through the windshield.

"Let's go home, you little shit-ass kid."

Neither one of us said a word on the way home.

Daphne was a sophisticated young lady who blossomed early and tried on different boyfriends like a closet full of fashionable shoes. She had even dated Argent. After a while it became obvious, even with my social ineptitude, she was interested in me. I told Rudd about it.

"You've got to talk to her."

"What? On the phone?"

"No man. We're not little kids anymore. We're in high school. It's better to talk to a chick in person. We should go to her house. Right now."

"Are you kidding me? You want to go now? It'll be dark soon."

"Yeah, but it's Friday night. It's still early. Let's go."

We walked down Hanselman Street to the end of his block, turned left at the corner, passed the city garage, passed the railroad tracks, and crossed over the culvert at Bad Axe Creek.

Have I mentioned how my hometown got its name? It was near that spot, on a slough at the edge of the creek, where road surveyor, Rudolph Pabst, in 1861, found an axe with a broken handle *and a splintered head* at his camp site and named it Bad Axe Camp.

We followed the curve past the end of Whitlam going towards A&W and turned right onto her road. Buchner's house is at the edge of town where the city limit gives way to country. We walked on the gravel road, a farm field on one side, and modern ranch homes on the other. The whole stretch of road was heavily sprayed with brine to keep the dust down. Luke and I walked down the center of the road kicking bits of gravel. When we got to her house the garage door was open and both vehicles were gone. As we walked across the front lawn a light came on and shined through an undraped bedroom window.

Luke stopped, held his index finger to his lips, and said, "Shhh."

"What?"

"Daphne just walked into the room."

"Really? You saw her?"

"Yeah."

Hiding in the shrubs at the edge of the brick house we grabbed the masonry ledge and lifted ourselves to the window for a better view. It wasn't Daphne, but my disappointment faded when her friend, Marla, removed her blue towel and stood completely naked looking in the mirror and brushing her hair. Completely naked!

"Holy shit, Luke."

"I know! I know! Would you look at those tits!"

She hung the towel on the doorknob and put on flannel pajamas. After brushing her hair again, she turned off the light, and left the room.

Luke said, "Holy crap!"

"I know, man – we've got to get out of here."

"No. Let's wait a minute."

"What are you, nuts?"

"No, we've got to wait. Where do you think Daphne is?"

"I don't know," I said. "Oh, yeah!"

We were still crouching in the shadows when the

bedroom light came on again. We grabbed the ledge, pulled ourselves up to the window, and pressed our feet against the red brick wall. We peeked into the window and there she was. She was wearing nothing but a towel around her body and one wrapped around her head. What color were the towels? I have no idea.

She removed the towel from her head, dried her hair, and brushed her long locks. When she removed the second towel, I saw a girl who wasn't a girl anymore. *She was there. She was all there. Mama jugs a plenty.* I couldn't believe what I was seeing. Standing there in awe, I couldn't believe that Daphne liked me. But she did, she did like me. This young woman, naked before my eyes, was interested in me.

Rudd and I watched her dry off and get dressed. The whole thing lasted only a couple of seconds, but those few moments were forever burned into my memory. She got dressed in pink and purple harlequin shorts, a navy t-shirt, and left the room.

"We got to get out of here, Luke."

"No. Let's wait. You came here to talk to Daphne, so talk to her. I'm here to make sure you do."

"You're crazy. We have to leave. Now."

"No Kubacki, you have to talk to her. That's why you came here. Talk to her, man."

"All right, all right. You're right. I'll talk to her."

We stayed crouched in the bushes for a few minutes until Luke nudged me toward the front steps. I went up the stairs and knocked on the screen door. The light metal door rattled but no one answered.

"Try the inside door."

I rapped on the wood door, a bit harder this time.

We heard voices and scampering feet from inside the house.

A lone voice shouted from an open window, "Who the hell is out there?"

Someone came to the door and the heavy slab slowly creaked open.

Daphne's friend Marla said, "Oh my God! What are you guys doing here?"

"I came here to see Daphne."

Marla moved to the side and Daphne stepped to the door.

"Were you guys here a minute ago?"

"No. We just got here."

Luke smiled, but didn't say anything.

"Oh, good."

I couldn't believe it. She was wearing some guy's football jersey with his name and number in yellow block letters stamped on it. She was dating some jock! So what? I was the one talking to Daphne right now, here on her front porch. I was sure I could win her over and have her as my girlfriend, a steady rollin' woman, all to myself.

Daphne and I talked for a few minutes and then Luke and I went home.

The Buchners usually went to eleven o'clock Mass on Sunday. My family liked sleeping in on Sunday – we attended Saturday evening service. While the rest of the family slept in, I started going to church on Sunday, *by myself.* I used to avoid going to church by any means possible. I hid under my bed, behind the water softener, under the basement stairs, or in the most obvious place, my tree fort.

I had to do something practical in case the love charms Dion and I cast failed to work. We found the spell in a magic book from the public library. Going to Mass was probably more effective than white magic to win her over. I started getting up early to go church on Sunday. I'd shit, shower, and shave, put on some good clothes, and ride my bike to church.

One day, I arrived at church and walked in using the side entrance near the altar – to make sure Daphne would see me coming in. I had sat through almost the entire Mass, over fifty minutes of sitting, standing, and kneeling, when I started to feel restless. I got up from the pew and walked out of the church. As I was heading to the bike rack someone flew out after me.

He ran to me, a well-manicured tuft of furious red hair, a blur of black, and a bouncing white collar. It was Father Eoch. He had been in the sacristy praying while Father Joe said Mass. I'm sure Eoch is the angriest person to ever wear a priest's vestments, and Lord, was he pissed-off at me.

Eoch drove a big yellow Cadillac. He also enjoyed spending time on the golf course and drinking whiskey at the clubhouse. Being a proud Irishman, he had changed the name of our humble church to The Kirk of the Thumb. Our parish was full of lots of Germans and Pollacks and his new moniker didn't go over well. The parishioners wanted to keep the name Sacred Heart Church.

Eoch grabbed my shoulder and said, "Young man, you left before Mass was finished."

"The service was over."

"Father Joe hasn't made the final blessing."

"But I have to get home before noon."

"That is no excuse. We don't leave before Mass is over. The final blessing is the most important part of the service. You ought to know better than that."

With God Himself backing him, he grabbed my left ear, dragged me into the foyer, and let go of me at the holy water font. He dipped his hand into the cup and crossed himself and I dipped my hand in the stale water and made the sign of the cross too. I didn't have a choice with the entire congregation, especially Daphne, watching. Eoch ushered me to an empty pew, and he stood beside me singing loudly, as I sang along, until the last moaning notes of the pipe organ stopped. She had seen the whole thing.

After school a few days later, I was climbing the box elder maple in our front yard. I was sitting in the tree staring up at the green canopy when I heard bicycles coming down the street. I looked down and saw two girls from school. It was Daphne and a one of her friends, Amy. I climbed down from the tree, stood at the end of our driveway, and watched the girls ride onto our front sidewalk. The girls were tittering, but they stopped giggling, and parked their bikes.

"Hi Daphne, what are you two doing here?"

Her friend Amy smiled and said hello.

"We were at the ballpark – it was kind of boring. We decided to take a ride around the block. Is this your house?"

"Yeah, this is my place." *She already knew.*

"And that's the tree fort I've heard about."

"You girls want to see it?"

"No. Maybe some other time. We have to get going."

"All right, I'll see ya later."

The next day, I looked Daphne up in the phone book and gave her a call.

Even though I wasn't interested in playing video games anymore, I was hanging out with my buddies in the arcade tent at the county fair. I still enjoyed watching them play the damn things. Luke was playing Asteroids, shooting up chunks of space debris and flying saucers. A stack of quarters sat on the sloped edge of the machine. I jostled the quarters in my pocket and watched the black and white screen as polygonal rocks floated through outer space.

After the arcade, we went exploring the midway. The gaming booths were in the center of the grounds with food concessions and carnival rides around the perimeter. We saw a bunch of people clustered around a new game of chance operating that year. It was really something.

All four sides of the trailer were lined with sparkling glass cases, each one littered with thousands of shiny quarters. Several thousand dollars right in front of your face. A small bar passed back and forth between the stacks of coins and pushed the quarters closer and closer to the edge. When the coins fell over the edge they dropped into a collection cup where the player received their cash prize. If you could drop your quarters in a good spot the bar would push a pile of coins into the cup.

The game looked easy enough. My friends and I played for about an hour but we really didn't win anything at all. We were lucky if we broke even. I saw lots of people dumping quarters into the fancy glass tanks, but no one got any big pay outs. Occasionally a few quarters slipped over the edge. We were wasting our time and our quarters, so we moved on.

At the next booth, the carnie performed a perfect demonstration for every potential contestant at the game. It immediately caught my attention. The object was to carefully drop five metal discs from a foot above a painted circle and completely cover the circle with the discs. The guy who ran the game must've practiced a million times, had memorized a secret pattern or like all the games on the midway it was rigged. I think he had a handful of slightly bigger discs to demonstrate how easy it was to win. I played the game, spent several dollars, lost every time, and walked away.

It was the same with marksmanship games, everything was rigged *for you to lose.* The machine BB guns you used to shoot out the entire paper star target weren't maintained properly. The rapid firing guns were old, worn out, underpowered, and didn't shoot straight.

If you were shooting darts the tips were dull, the shafts bent, the balloons underinflated or made of heavy latex that wouldn't easily pop. It was impossible to find sharp tips, so when I played darts, I looked at all the darts and picked three with the straightest shafts. I aimed carefully, threw the projectile with force, and hoped the thick rubber balloon would pop.

The dart game I liked best didn't have stupid stuffed animals as prizes. You played to win decorative mirrors instead.

They had tiny purse sized mirrors, reputedly preferred by coke heads, big wall mount mirrors, and several sizes in between. After your first win, you got the coke mirror, and with each consecutive win, you moved up to larger and larger mirrors. I shot through the small prizes and worked up to the twelve-inch mirrors and won several of the LP sized ones painted with album cover art from my favorite rock bands.

My buddies and I walked away from the shooting gallery to grab some Gibby's Fries and a Coke. Before we reached the concession trailer, I saw Daphne and her friends walking towards us. We stopped and chatted with the girls. My buddies took off to get their junk food and I went with Daphne, Marla, and Amy.

Daphne wanted to see what mirrors I'd won. I showed them to her. She liked the mirrors, but after seeing which albums they featured, she wrinkled her nose. "You have some interesting taste in music. Those bands are a bit too heavy for me, and Pink Floyd is not one my favorites, either. But I saw a Def Leppard mirror, maybe you could win one of those for me."

"I can't stand Def Leppard. They're awful. But I'll win a mirror for you."

I shot one round of darts and won a coke mirror. Did it two more times and worked up to a twelve-inch for my girl. Afterward, we walked around the midway and talked. I was enjoying myself and the company of Daphne and her girlfriends.

When Pink Floyd's movie, *The Wall,* debuted, a

bunch of people went to Saginaw to see it. I didn't go because it was too far to drive and didn't have a license anyway. When it finally came to Bad Axe, a huge line formed on opening night. The long lines formed again, and again, for weeks after coming to town. It was amazing, everybody in Huron County must have seen it. The line stretched along the front sidewalk, wrapped around the corner, and down the block to the next corner. The line went nearly halfway around the block. There hadn't been this kind of turn out for a movie since *Star Wars.*

Daphne asked me to see *The Wall* with her. She didn't like Pink Floyd, yet she wanted to see the movie. *I knew she was into me.*

"You want to go see that movie?"

"Yes, on a date. Dinner might be too much but we could stop for fries and a shake at McDonald's and then go to the movie."

"I thought you didn't like Floyd."

"They're not my favorite. But I heard the movie is well done. Mr. North recommended it. Remember? My friend Greta wants to see it too. She can drive and go with us." Daphne was thoughtful enough to keep her mom, or Charlene, from tagging along to chaperone, and had arranged transportation with her friend.

When we went out, I could tell Daphne was bored with the movie. At least Greta enjoyed it, and like me, she could hardly take her eyes off the silver screen.

After the movie we stopped at Greta's house to check in with her parents. While she was inside, Daphne came on to me. Quietly and forcefully, she pressed her lips to mine and we started to make out. No pecks on the lips or anything simple, we dove straight into some heated French kissing. After a few minutes of smacking lips and heavy breathing, I worked up the courage to head for second base – now that I knew what it was. I reached into her sweater and managed to undo the complicated bra clip. As soon as I undid the clasp, the sling fell forward from the weight of her wonderful breasts. I had developed a preference for champagne breasts, but her big set of D-cups *were fine with me.*

We hadn't drunk any beer, booze, or wine, but I felt intoxicated. I was sexually excited like never before. This felt great because this was something I wanted. Now that I knew what I really wanted. I wanted her. I don't remember getting dropped off at home. My head was too high in the clouds.

We didn't go on another date. Instead, I started riding my bike to Daphne's neighborhood to hang out at Marla's house. Her mom was never home. They had a finished basement and a huge TV with surround sound. I liked hanging out *with a bunch of girls,* and when Daphne and I were alone, even for a few seconds, we necked and fondled each other. When Marla, or Daphne's younger sister, came back downstairs, they'd catch us with our lips locked and my hands under Daphne's blouse. I tried reaching into her harlequin shorts several times, but I didn't even get close to third base. But it didn't matter, I was the only dude there, and I felt like a king.

Daphne started calling me Little Bucka because she said I was a lot like my old man. She said I looked like my dad and rode my bike everywhere like him too. He did ride his bike, rain, shine, or snow, up-and-down our block, to and from work, five, sometimes six days a week. But looking back now, I suspect Daphne knew something about me that I wasn't aware of then. My *temperament* was like Buckley's too.

Daphne was smart, pretty, and I had her for keeps. She used those other boys to figure out what she wanted in a guy – she wanted a guy like me – and I wasn't about to let her go. She helped me learn how to be comfortable around girls. How to French kiss. She let me get to second base. And, I reclaimed some of my manhood I had lost being Coby's bitch.

I didn't talk to that asshole for five or six years until I saw him at a party down the road from Rolnik's farm during Christmas break from college. He was hanging out with his jock buddies from high school. I was embarrassed and worried to see him there. Embarrassed and worried that I might cause a scene or that he might cause a scene. Everyone there would find out about our fucked-up childhood secrets. Instead, we looked at each other and mumbled something like, "How you doing, man?" "Not bad, how are you doing?"

We gave each other a pass.

Grandpa Booms and many of my uncles, including my Godfather, Uncle Rusty, smoked pipes. Mom said her dad used to smoke cigarettes and drink whiskey before he took up pipes and beer. Grandpa used to give Mom a penny for each ash tray she emptied. Before he switched to beer, he was a different kind of drinker.

After a bad argument, Grandma rounded up her young kids, got in the car, and drove off to get away from him. Grandma drove a few miles down the road, pulled into a tractor lane at the edge of a field, and sat there for twenty minutes watching the crops grow. A few cars drove by and she decided to head home before some busybody neighbors started asking nosy questions.

The next day when Grandpa sobered up, Grandma insisted they visit the parish priest in Port Hope, not their own priest at Our Lady of Lake Huron, to maintain their privacy.

"Bernard, what do you think you can do to make things better for your wife and kids?"

Grandpa thought for a minute, said his drinking was out of hand, and told the priest he would have to quit.

Grandpa never quit. He couldn't. But he switched exclusively to beer. That's what I remember him drinking. Cases of empty brown bottles were all over the basement and on the bench in his work shop. *I guess that priest must've put the fear of God into him.* He also quit cigarettes and started puffing on corncob pipes in the barn and fields, cheap drugstore briars in the house, and a beautiful white meerschaum every now and then.

A lot of people smoked tobacco when I was a kid. Even if they didn't have the habit a lot of men smoked cigars on special occasions, those cheap ones with a pink or blue paper ring handed out by some proud papa. A lot of men, and *scandalously* a lot of women, smoked cigarettes. My parents tried cigarettes too, but they didn't have the urge to keep smoking.

I can imagine Mom and a bunch of her friends at nursing school sneaking a smoke on campus. Mom probably took one puff, felt an instant rush of dizziness, and knew right away she wasn't a smoker. And Dad smoked cigarettes in the Army with his bunkmates in Alaska, to fit in with the boys, but didn't pick up the habit.

I loved the way Mom and Dad smelled, covered in stale smoke, when they came home from bowling. Mom didn't like when people smoked but let her friend Lana, an older colleague from the hospital, get away with sneaking a smoke in our bathroom. Her cigarette butts wouldn't flush down after she dropped one in the toilet. They were always floating around in the bowl until they became soggy enough to go down the drain.

Back then, smoking in a restaurant, bar, break room at work, and even the teachers' lounge was permitted. It's no wonder I wanted to try smoking, nearly everybody smoked, and a lot of my buddies wanted to try it too.

I stole my first real pack of cigarettes from Mr. Kole. A pack of cigarettes unlike any pack of smokes I'd seen before. It was a thin box with a flip-top and contained a single row of seven cigarettes. He'd gotten several sample packs from a tobacco company eager to gain new customers. Tobacco had already enchanted me and when I saw this unique packaging I had to take one. After eating snacks with Mason, I grabbed one of the packs from the countertop, took it home, and hid it in my tree fort.

Before I stashed them, I tore off the cellophane wrapper and carefully opened the box. A deep smell of hay, a slight tinge of burning autumn leaves, and a heavy, but pleasant mint aroma rushed up my nose. I didn't smoke them right away – I had to wait to share them with my friends.

Later that week, I told Argent and Dion about the cigarettes. We smoked two of them in the fort. The nude pin-ups watched with wanton looks as if they were asking, "Why aren't you boys sharing your sexy cigarettes with us?" I lit the first cigarette, took a deep drag, and handed it to Argent. Tom took a puff and his ashy skin became even paler. Dion lit the second cigarette and slowly inhaled the luscious smoke as if he knew what he was doing.

I lit up a Swisher Sweet Dion had taken from his grandpa's milkhouse and inhaled the wretched smoke. It swirled around inside my lungs and made my heart beat faster. My head wobbled and my arms turned into rubber. Mom was right, this shit does make you dizzy. Dion took a few puffs of the Swisher and snuffed out the stinky thing. Tom had had enough to smoke. Dion and I finished the cigarettes.

The following weekend we smoked in my fort again. We had stolen some Swishers and a packet of pipe tobacco from the drugstore but we didn't have a pipe. We weren't able to steal one because they were behind the counter. But the lack of paraphernalia didn't stop us, we made our own pipe instead. Crafted it from a piece of scrap pine wood which still had a coat of varnish from its previous life as a decorative newel on the brick planter in our living room. Dion and I made the pipe from the pine by drilling out the inside of the bowl, shaping the outside of the bowl on Dad's bench grinder, smoothing the whole piece with a scrap of old sandpaper, and attaching fish tank airline. It looked like a badly made hookah.

Dion, Tom, and I sat on the floor of the fort around our pipe. It was hard to light the moist tobacco but we finally got it going. We passed the tubing around and puffed on the homemade hookah. Argent tried it, coughed, and passed it to Dion. Argent didn't want any more, so Dion and I passed it back and forth until the bowl was spent.

I was smoking a cigarette with Rudd one day. He had been smoking for some time and gave me some suggestions. Luke told me I should stop shaving my mustache, don't shave for a couple of days, then go to the store to buy smokes. When you're in the store, don't shop around, don't buy a candy bar, a pop, or bring *anything* to the checkout.

"Walk up to the counter, look the cashier in the eye, politely smile, and ask for a pack of Marlboro Reds in a box, please. They won't even card ya."

He was right.

Eight

One day after school, I came into the house and bounded down the stairs to my room. The door was open and lights were on. I stood in front of the desk and noticed my box was unlocked, open, and completely empty. My stash was gone. *Which one of my buddies took my magazines?* I sat at my desk wondering who did it.

I was going upstairs to grab a snack. As I approached the stairs, I saw Charlene sitting in front of the wood furnace with the door open. She was picking up schnitzels of paper and throwing them into the fire. As she stoked the furnace, I noticed an unusual look on her face. In the dim light of the fire her face seemed to be full of fear. I saw a stack of magazines sitting on the floor next to the scraps of cardboard and paper. She picked up a magazine, threw it in the fire, and then I realized what they were.

Busted!

"Charlene, what are you doing?"

"I'm getting rid of your filthy magazines. Where the heck did you get so many?"

"It's none of your business."

"What's wrong with you, Stephen Mark? Is this what you think women look like? This is not how women act. Real women don't touch themselves like that."

I screamed at her, "You're wrong! Dead wrong! My girlfriends think the photography is beautiful, and real women do touch themselves like that. It's called masturbation and it doesn't give you hairy palms or make you go blind. I know because I read it in those magazines *and your sex education book.*"

I went upstairs and ran out the back door. I needed to get away from her. Needed to be somewhere she couldn't get me. Needed to be in my tree fort. The rope ladder was pulled up inside the fort, and the wood ladder was drawn up too. I scaled the trunk of the tree, opened the trap door, and crawled inside. I slammed the door to the floor and bolted the lock.

When I was in grade school, a lot of kids cut through the block across the street from the elementary school. Cutting through sheared fifteen minutes off a thirty-minute walk. Almost all the kids living south of the school did it. With all the kids cutting through the back yards, and not many adults watching, it was a good spot for an after-school fight. When I saw a fight, I did one of two things. If the fight involved two boys my age I stopped and egged them on with the other kids. If it involved boys older than me, I used a different path, sneaked through the block, and avoided a possible confrontation with them.

Kids also cut through the church parking lot next to the school. You cut through the church lot, ran down the hill, and held your breath to avoid the stink from the laundromat waste water pond.

The Wash King had two coin-operated vending machines. One sold chips and candy, operated by pulling a lever, which sent your snack down a metal ramp. The other machine had ice cold pop. It released a shiny glass bottle from its spot, you took out a bottle, and the next one rolled into the empty slot. Both machines ate lots of my lunch money. I drank the pop on the way to school and saved some of the junk food for lunch.

A lot of older boys stopped at the laundromat to pick up snacks. They stole lunch money from me and my friends. After a while, Coby, Stosh, and I knew exactly when they'd show up. We started going to school early to hit the vending machines. Sometimes, to avoid them, we went to the old Sunoco garage because the gas station also sold candy bars, chips, and pop. High school age boys, who didn't bully us, and the old farts from around town hung out there smoking cigarettes, cheap cigars, and shooting the shit.

Snock used the shortcut by the laundromat too. He tried to stop us from cutting through the church parking lot one day.

A lot of kids picked on the weirdo. I think everyone in Bad Axe knew about him and what he did to younger kids. I remembered the dirty stuff he had done to us, but I had repressed the memory of him threatening to kill me.

Snock was a strange kid. He was always doing weird things. Crashing his bike into trees. Riding his bike off a Little League dugout and breaking his fucking leg. And the fucked-up stuff that no one ever tried to stop. Bullying kids a few years younger than him, threatening them, molesting them. The sad thing is somebody probably abused Bentley. Nobody tried to help him and he kept tampering with kids in town. The town kept *giving him a pass.* He didn't *need a pass.* He needed help.

One day after leaving the elementary school, Bentley stopped us at the edge of the church parking lot in front of a huge forsythia hedge at the top of the laundromat hill. He had stepped out from behind the shrubs, stopped us in our tracks, and grabbed the handlebars of my bike.

"You guys can't ride your bikes through here anymore. This is private property."

"What do you mean? This is the church parking lot. You don't own it."

"I go to church here. It's my church and I'm saying you guys can't cut through."

"Why the hell not? Everyone cuts through here. Just like everyone cuts through our trail to the fairgrounds. Screw you, Bent-knee Fuck!"

Coby said, "Why don't you go get bent, Bent?"

And Zee added, "Yeah, man, Snock you!"

Kids in Bad Axe were always cutting through people's yards and traipsing around where they shouldn't. As my friends and I got older, even in junior high and high school, we didn't stop. We kept taking shortcuts through anyone's yard, everywhere we went, anytime we wanted.

During seventh and eighth grade, Dion and I cut through the alley behind Huron Music almost every day. We used a well-worn path through the thick hedge between the alley and the back yards on the block. We went down Spears's driveway, crossed Woodworth Street, and walked to Argent's house. One day when cutting through, we noticed something we hadn't noticed before. There were several trash bags full of aluminum cans sitting on Spears's garage floor.

Dion said, "Holy crap, look at all those empties!"

"Imagine if we could cash those in. How much would that be worth?"

After leaving Argent's house, Dion and I walked down Spears's driveway on the way back to my place. Passing the open garage, we looked at each other, shrugged our shoulders, went in, and took four bags of empty cans. The bags reeked of stale beer. It was all beer cans. We returned them at the party store next to the arcade and bought a bunch of junk food, a couple of pops, and kept the rest of the money for later.

The following day, a Bad Axe cop pulled into my driveway as we were sitting down for supper. The cop got out of the cruiser, put on his flat-topped cap, and walked across the lawn to the front steps.

Officer Wayne Valentine was no detective, just a good-old-boy traffic cop who liked to drink beer on the weekends. In this particular case, no detective work was needed. He had talked to Mr. Spears about the stolen cans. After talking to Spears, Valentine probably thought of visiting several stores, but had gone to the nearest one – like we had – and solved the crime on the spot. Every can we had returned was Miller Lite, Mr. Spears's favorite, and the store clerks remembered us and knew me by name.

On my parents' front porch, Valentine explained the situation to Bucka and Charlie. They were pissed off. Man, were they pissed! Mom made a call to Grace.

"Our boys have been up to some mischief."

I rode with Bucka and Charlene as we followed the cop to Dion's.

Grace answered the door with the palm of her hand under her chin, fingertips resting on her lips. Valentine told her the story and explained what happened. He said Dion and I were under suspicion of breaking and entering and there was enough evidence to charge us.

Dion said, "Why are we being charged with a B & E? We didn't break into anything. The garage door was wide open. The cans were sitting by the door. We didn't break and enter. We walked in and took them."

Valentine looked at us, smiled, and offered a suggestion.

Grace looked up the number in the Yellow Pages and picked up the phone to call the Spears. She spun the numbers on the rotary dial, click-click-click, spoke for several seconds, and gave the phone to Officer Valentine. The cop spoke for a minute, nodded his head, said uh-huh a few times, and placed the handset on its cradle.

"Mr. Spears wants a formal apology for what you two did. He also expects you to reimburse him for the empties. He's decided to not file charges, and if you satisfy his conditions, I won't file charges either."

The whole thing was cleared up with a single phone call.

Officer Valentine then told us the specifics of breaking and entering, and besides the B & E, we had stolen goods, and trespassed on private property. He reminded us he could still file charges but wouldn't if we complied with Mr. Spears's demands.

He gave us a pass.

My parents didn't drink much. They limited their drinking to a toast at holiday meals, enjoying a glass of wine with dinner. That was enough for them. But they had two cupboards in the basement full of homemade wine and booze. Buck made his hooch from grapes, dandelions, marigolds, rose petals, or any other thing he could ferment in his black and tan crock. He made gallons of wine every year.

Bucka's been making wine for as long as I can remember. He always had some fruit or flower concoction fermenting in the basement. He used a fifty-five-gallon ceramic crock to prepare a batch. Bucka dumped water, a few cups of sugar for fruit wines, or several pounds for flower wines, into the crock. He let the brew sit for weeks, foaming and frothing. Mother Nature turns water into wine just like Jesus did. The crock stank up the whole basement as it fermented. When it was ready, Dad decanted the wine into one-gallon glass jugs by carefully pouring it through layers of cheese cloth set in a funnel. He fitted the big bottles with small p-traps and burp-balloons to regulate gas exchange and let them work though a second fermentation as they sat on top of the big oak desk.

He kept his wine in a special cupboard in the basement where they stored our home canned food. My friends and I drank straight out of the bottles whenever we wanted. No one ever noticed. There were tons of bottles, I could take one, *or four,* and the old man didn't know any were missing. Mom gave the stuff away once in a while but Dad used it as currency. He gave his wine to lots of people. If my old man owed you a favor, he returned the favor but he also gave you some hooch. A bottle or two would magically appear on your front porch or in your garage with a thank you note attached.

One morning before school, I got drunk on his grape wine. I had grabbed a large plastic tumbler from my desk, opened the cupboard, and poured myself some homemade vino. The cup was half empty when Dad came downstairs to see if I was ready for breakfast. I didn't think he would notice what I was drinking because the stuff looks exactly like our homemade grape juice.

But he noticed the smell, or maybe he noticed the dark purple fluid clinging like oil to the side of the plastic cup. He took the drink from me, held it to his nose, and took a good sniff. He shot a serious look at me.

"I needed to relax this morning."

"Oh, Steve. Your Grandma Lucy caught me drinking her homemade wine one day, like you are now."

Buck told me the questions Grandma K had asked him when he got caught drinking her homemade vino back on the farm.

"How often do you drink my wine? What will happen when you need more and you need to drink every day? What if there's none left in the cellar? What will you do then, Buckley?"

I went to school drunk that day but stopped drinking in the morning after that. But I didn't stop stealing Bucka's best for my buddies and me to drink on Friday nights. I was a typical teenager out partying with my friends. I wasn't using a crutch. I was only having some fun. After all, boys just want to have fun.

A few months earlier, in July or August, we started band practice. Marching in high school was a lot more fun than junior high, but also a lot more work. We marched around the bus lanes that wrapped around the football field, and then stomped back to the practice football field behind the intermediate school. Our parade skills were fine, but we needed to work on our choreography for half-time shows and marching band competitions.

Mr. North had arranged several pieces of popular music for the band. *Dueling Banjos, Georgia on My Mind, Hard to Say I'm Sorry,* and *Get Away.*

Dueling Banjos was renamed *Dueling Sawicki's* because Fran and Vesna Sawicki battled each other on glockenspiel, instead of banjos, while the rest of the band stopped playing and acted strictly as color guard.

The school bought a special insurance policy for my trombone, and all the other instruments, because we threw our horns in the air like batons. The color guard threw their flags at us and we threw our instruments to them, back and forth, in a spectacular volley. Only one instrument hit the ground the entire season. Insurance paid the claim for the player's banged-up trumpet.

The drummers needed to work out some issues while the angel trumpets and devil trombones rested. North and both drum majors hashed out the specifics of cadences, flams, and rolls with the drum section. As they hammered it out on snares, toms, bass drums, and cymbals, the rest of the band sat down, chatted, and listened to them struggle with the complicated rhythms.

Brian Cooper, a senior who played a silver two-valve trombone – he hardly ever touched his slide – walked over to chat with the Sawicki sisters. Dion, Tom, Luke, Ronnie, and I were hanging out with the girls. I thought Cooper was coming to talk to the ladies, but he walked directly toward me. He pointed at me and pressed his finger into my chest.

"Hey, you're that kid. You're that kid with the freaky eyes. You got freaky eyes, man!"

"What are you talking about, Cooper?"

"Your eyes, man. They're freaky."

"I'm not sure what you mean. My eyes are bright blue. So what? Sometimes, I wear two different colored contacts. You're probably noticing that."

"No. It's something else. You always look spaced out. Like you're high on something."

But I was never drunk at practice, it was impossible to march drunk, and hadn't even tried drugs yet.

North finished yelling at the drummers and the drum majors called the band to attention. A trombonist a year ahead of me said, "Let's go, *Chewbocki!*" The band fell into neat rows and columns, formed a perfect rectangle, and marched back to the school in parade formation to the sound of a single dry drum.

Tap. Tap. P-tap, tap, tap.

One Friday after school, I was in a rush to get home. I needed a quick shower before changing into my band uniform for the football game. We were going to perform our entire marching set during halftime and blast *Let's Go Blue* while the Hatchets played. I was strutting down the hall to the fishbowl at the front door when I saw my girl.

She was wearing a two-toned, leather sleeved jacket. It looked a size too big for her. As she came through the crowded hall, I realized she was being escorted by a senior. Her elbow was locked in his. The big frumpy thing she had on was his varsity jacket. *Not another jock.* The guy looked at me, my face twisted, Daphne looked at me and said, "Oh crap."

"Daphne? What the hell are you doing with him? Stupid fucking jock!"

They turned away and headed to the door. As they walked through the doorway, Daphne looked back at me, tossed her hair over her shoulder, and said, "I'm sorry, Steve," and walked into the parking lot.

Daphne was gone. I was crushed.

Later that week, after Mom's spaghetti for dinner, I was sitting on my mattress, wearing headphones, listening to music at maximum volume. I didn't hear someone knocking on the back door, didn't hear them come into the house, and didn't hear them bounding down the stairs. The doorknob turned, the door opened, and there was Luke. I took off my headphones.

"Hey, Luke. What's going on?"

"How are you man?"

I told him about seeing Daphne and her football player, asshole boyfriend. Luke said we should go for a walk and stop at the arcade that had recently opened near the junior high. Anthony Marks old man owned the place. Rudd said they had just got in a bunch of new video games.

"We should go check them out."

"Yeah, it might take my mind off of her."

We walked down South Street towards the baseball park. As we passed the Little League fields, Luke pulled out a small bottle hidden inside his coat pocket. An ice-cold bottle of peppermints schnapps. Because the ball fields are across the street from the county jail we ducked into one of the dugouts by the softball diamond facing away from the clink.

Luke cracked the seal on the clear liquor bottle. He took a snort and handed it to me. I took a huge gulp.

"Whoa, take it easy, save some for me."

"Thanks, man. That's fucking good!"

We passed the bottle back and forth until it was gone. As we walked away, I said, "I can't believe we drank a pint that fast."

Luke laughed at me and said, "That was a fifth, Kubacki."

"Are you shitting me?"

"I shit you not."

I had hit the bottle hard and had drunk over half a fifth of peppermint schnapps.

We walked by the county jail and courthouse on the way to the arcade. When we got there, I was completely shit-faced and started making an ass of myself. I said rude, outrageous things and yelled profanities at people. You would have to ask them what I said because I have no idea. But I do remember crashing into a glass display case and jostling the merchandise inside. My buddy, Tony, who was working the joint for his old man got pissed off at me.

"Hey, take it easy, Kubacki! You're wrecking the

display." I mumbled something to him and crashed into the case again. Marks gave me a sore looked and started reorganizing the buttons and other crap inside the case.

Someone ordered Little Caesars pizza. When it arrived, everyone at the arcade scarfed down a few pieces. Having the munchies from drinking too much booze I ate several pieces and ate it too fast. *It must have been delicious.*

I have no memory of walking home, but that's what I did, walk home – somehow – with Rudd's help. I could never have made it myself. I could barely stand let alone walk. I don't know if Luke delivered me to the back door or if he left me at the edge of our yard to avoid talking to my parents. But I went into the house and made it downstairs without saying hello to the anyone.

It was a school night and the family was probably sitting in front of the idiot box. Nobody saw me come in as I stumbled downstairs to my room. I crawled onto my mattress on the floor and passed into a shallow sleep.

A short time later, I woke up retching. I was still weak from my drunken stupor and couldn't make it to the bathroom in time. I grabbed a yellow plastic trash can covered in Budweiser Racing stickers to catch the toxic mix of spaghetti dinner, minty schnapps, and cheap pizza flowing from my mouth. For months afterwards, I was unable to eat Italian food, and to this day I'm not fond of anything peppermint.

The next morning Buckley woke me earlier than usual – before waking Jacob, Contessa, and Wren – to chat with me about the wonderful evening I'd had.

The evening's the great time, isn't it, little Stevie, boy?

"You must've had some kind of good time last night, huh?"

"I feel like shit, Bucka."

"Well, you upchucked everything you put into yourself."

"I feel sick, Dad. I can't go to school."

"You get in that shower and get dressed. Now!"

"I'm not going to school today."

"You're probably not fit for breakfast, but you're going to school, you shit-ass kid."

I got in the shower, sat on the stall floor, bathed myself, and went to school in a half-drunken stupor.

Sawicki's family traveled to Poland that summer. They were going to meet some distant relatives and figure out how the branches of their family tree connected. They would be gone for two or three weeks and needed someone to keep an eye on the place and bring in the mail. Mr. Sawicki asked my buddy Dion to look after things while they were away.

One evening, my friends and I were walking to the drugstore when Dion said, "Hey guys, I have to go to Sawicki's and get their mail after we get done here."

While my pals looked in the cooler, I shopped the tobacco and wine aisle. I spotted the perfect sized bottle, knew it would fit, slipped the cheap wine down the front of my pants, and walked outside. I waited at the side of the building and smoked a cigarette.

Tom and Dion came outside laughing their asses off. Dion removed a pack of cigars from his inside coat pocket and shouted, “Woo-hoo!”

I said, “Oh yeah?” And removed the bottle of Mad Dog from my coat. The wine was well concealed and my friends didn’t know I had stolen it.

Dion said, “You fucking dog!”

“All right, man! That’s some shit.”

We ran across Port Crescent to the sidewalk on the other side of the street. We walked down a side street, through the Lutheran church parking lot, climbed a fence into the adjacent yard, cut through, and came out onto the sidewalk. We walked a few yards on the cement path and cut into another yard. We drank, smoked, and trespassed all the way to Sawicki’s.

Tom and I waited while Dion got Sawicki’s mail. Dion returned with a stack of junk mail and bills. We clamored up the side porch, Dion removed the key from his pocket and opened the door. Tom and I came up behind him as he entered the house.

He said, “I’ll be right back you guys,” and slipped inside the door to put the mail on the kitchen table. Dion came out a few minutes later sporting a huge smile under his large glasses and three cans of cold beer in his hands.

“Beer scam!”

“All right, Dion!”

“Oh, man.”

We already had the crappy drugstore wine but isn’t beer always better? We stood around drinking our beers, passing the bottle of wine, and smoking cigars and cigarettes. The booze was soon gone. We smoked some more and talked. I was staring into space when Dion asked, "You guys want to go swimming? Frances said we could use the pool."

The suggestion of cool water on a hot summer night sent us scrambling to the back yard. Dion and I peeled back the floating tarp and folded it in half to create an open area to swim. We stripped off our clothes in seconds.

Dion and Tom knew how to swim, but I didn't, I faked it. At the lake, in shallow water, I used my hands to crawl along the sandy bottom while floating on the surface. It looked kind of like swimming and I thought no one would know the difference. I could only dive and propel myself underwater by kicking.

I dived to the bottom of the pool, kicked like a bitch, and pushed myself to the surface. There wasn't room for laps around the small pool, we could only swim back and forth inside the open half of the pool.

Stopping for a rest, we leaned against the pool's edge and reached into the garden for a few perfectly ripe raspberries. The bushes grew up to the top of the swimming pool. Sweet corn was tasseling out and the season's first tomatoes were blushing with spots of red. We ate a few more handfuls of berries and went back to swimming.

I dove under and stayed down for as long as possible. I waited too long, felt burning in my lungs, and needed to come up for air. I pushed up and reached for the cool night air but couldn't catch my breath because I'd come up into a net. A thick net enclosing me. I didn't know what was happening.

What the hell are they trying to do to me? Why are they fucking around with me? They know I can't swim.

I struggled, rolled, and tried to break free from the net. Dion and Tom had thrown a net over me. But it wasn't a net, it was the pool cover. I had come up underneath the floating bubble wrap and was trapped. I couldn't fucking breathe. The plastic pushed me down as I tried to reach the surface.

Argent and Dion helped me get out of the tangled plastic and managed to get me out of the water. I'm damn sure they saved my life. I stood leaning against the rickety aluminum ladder and retched out some chlorinated water. I pulled myself up to the ladder, crawled through the handrails, flipped over the edge of the pool, and fell to the ground. Dion and Tom climbed out and stood above me. I got up from the ground. We wrung out our hair, shook the coppery water from our limbs, and got dressed.

I said, "Let's get the fuck out of here, guys."

Nine

In my sophomore year. on the first day of biology class, I found a seat next to my buddy, Ronnie Rolnik. Our teacher, Mr. Mustard, was explaining how he usually assigned lab partners. Then he said, “This year’s class has an even 50-50 male to female ratio. All lab partners will be boy-girl. You can pick your own partners.”

I became friends with Rolnik in third grade when Ronnie and I started sketching animal pictures from The World Book Encyclopedia – the A book. His family and mine owned the same set of books. I liked sleeping over at Ronnie’s house because he lived in the country on a dairy farm.

One spring, I spent a Friday and Saturday night at the Rolnik’s. Like many farmers, they consider water to be their most precious resource, and saving water any way possible is a way of life. To conserve water, Ronnie’s mom told us to take a shower together.

I was confused when he didn’t want to do anything with me in the shower, so I tried doing something to him. He shouted out in protest.

His mom yelled from the living room, “What are you boys doing in there?”

“Nothing, Mom.”

For Friday night dinner, since it was Lent, Mrs. Rolnik served sucker fish caught in the Pinnebog River, which meandered through their land. I refused to eat the ugly looking, funny smelling, smoked fish. Mr. Rolnik said an off-color remark about me not eating the fish.

“Is he some kind of sissy, Edie? The kid won’t eat

the fish."

"Leave the boy alone, Gilmore. His family probably doesn't eat sucker fish."

She made a box of macaroni and cheese and some frozen fish sticks for me to eat. For some reason, Ronnie and I didn't hang out much after that weekend.

A couple of cute girls were sitting in front of Ronnie and me. We asked them to partner with us. Rolnik didn't care which one, they were both pretty, but I had my eye on one of them. I asked her to be my lab partner and she agreed.

She was a year behind me, and had been since grade school, but unbelievably I had never noticed her before. She wore loud perfume and had big hair scrunched up high with half a can of hairspray.

After school, I looked Gretchen up in the Yellow Pages. There were three listings for Maddox in our small town's phone book. Two of the entries were addresses on the other side of town, too far away to walk to school, the third listing was an address on my side of town.

I made a plan.

I started walking home a different way to bump into Gretchen walking home from school. It happened within a week. I started bumping into her every day. I talked with her, walked her home, and one day worked up the nerve to ask her out.

Our first date late that fall was chaperoned by my buddy, Carson Eachagain. He was cool enough to drive us around Bad Axe. His younger sister, Sophie, came along with us. She and Gretchen had been friends since they were kids. It was weird going on a date with them tagging along, but having Sophie with us made conversation livelier. Carson said a buddy of his had hauled him around on his first date and didn't mind taking us out cruising. Gretchen and I sat in the back of his rusty green Vega while the Eachagains sat up front. We drove back and forth between the tractor dealer parking lot on the east end of town and McDonald's at the north end. All evening, we cruised town drinking beer and smoking cigarettes.

Carson and Sophie were probably glad to get rid of me when they dropped me off at home. They must have been tired of me making moves on Gretchen in the back seat. I wasn't even getting anywhere. Carson stopped the car in the street to let me off at the end of the driveway. I gave Gretchen an awkward kiss, crawled out of the back seat, and went inside pent up with mixed feelings of sexual excitement and frustration.

That winter, two days before Christmas, Dion, Argent, and I were hanging out downtown. It was the night of the Christmas parade which ran a few blocks from the east end by the junior high to the high school on the west side of Bad Axe. We were flipping through album bins at Huron Music when a clerk, a guy working during his break from University of Michigan, came over and said hello.

Zozecki said, "There's a good selection of classic rock right now."

Dion said, "I know, I can't believe it. You guys got

amazing stuff."

"Yeah, good stuff, Zozecki," I said, "this is great."

After an hour of browsing, we took our selections to the counter. Tom and Dion paid with cash. I asked for a store charge. The owner, Mr. Vivers, overheard, reached for a small metal recipe box, flipped through the tabs to K-L, and said, "He's got a small balance, but we can let Kubacki charge another one. He's good for it," he chuckled. "We know where he lives."

"All right, Vivers." Zozecki made notations on the 3-by-5 card and put it back in the box. "Thanks guys, I appreciate it." After bagging our purchases, he leaned in closer and said to us, "I don't know if you guys are interested, but I've got some sinsemilla. Really great kind bud."

Dion said, "No way, man."

I said, "Yeah, not our thing, Zozecki."

Tom stood back smiling, nodding his head.

We left the store through the back door and headed to Argent's house to check out our new vinyl. As we were cutting through Spears's yard, Tom stopped, looked at us, and said, "Hey guys, maybe we should try some of Zozecki's pot. It sounds as if he's got some good stuff. You can't find quality pot like that around here."

What?

Dion and I looked at Tom. We talked it over for a few minutes and decided, yes, it was time to try the devil's weed we had been warned about. Our parents had told us all about the burnouts in town. Buckley and Charlene had made legends of older kids on my block and their parties in the pot fort back in the woods.

They had a small Franklin stove, bunkbeds, *and electricity in their fort*. How could potheads be anything other than cool if they had built a set up like that?

We went back to the store, talked to Zozecki, and scored a big bag of fluffy, sticky weed. This stuff smelled amazing, like basil and oregano, but it also had a slightly urinous, skunky smell, with notes of pine and lemon. Not a single whiff of hay. I don't know how much we bought. Remembering the size of it now, probably a half ounce. It was a huge bag of pot – filled half a sandwich bag – we paid next to nothing for it, and there wasn't a single seed in that shit. Knowing what I know now, it was probably grown indoors in the attic of a rental house in Ann Arbor.

We bought a pack of Zig-Zags at the party store and made two poorly rolled joints in the parking lot. I lit one and Tom lit the other as we walked down the alley. The weed didn't smell like burning rope, it smelled fantastic. We passed the joints around until there were two tiny butts left. Tom told us to save the roaches. For about twenty minutes it had no effect. Disappointment could describe how I felt, but I didn't really know what would happen. Then slowly, I felt something creeping in me and it crawled up inside my brain.

Instead of going to Argent's, we walked to my house where everything became more interesting. We couldn't play our new LPs, so we listed to my cassettes. The music we had heard dozens of times before seemed sharper, the overtones more distinct, the sounds more sibilant. I noticed the red LED display on my alarm clock glowing, the small lights gently pulsed, vacillated, and then the clock's numbers started to roll like waves on the beach.

That Christmas, Argent's brother, Matt, came home on leave from Europe. His hair was clipped short in a rough buzzcut. It was great to see him even though he looked and acted differently.

Because he was a guitar player in the Marine Band, he was allowed to grow his hair to his shoulders and had avoided the clippers during his first year. But it grew too long for Uncle Sam. When it grew past his shoulders a superior officer ordered him to, "Go get your damn hair cut!"

Matt went to the barbershop for a trim. Since the barber only knew one style, he gave him a standard issue, all clipper, no guard, buzz cut. He was the same old Matt but more serious, more interesting, a lot smarter, and more fun to hang out with than before he enlisted.

Another day during the holiday break, I was at Huron Music looking in the album bins and Matt was there browsing too. A friend of his walked into the store. Pip told Matt his friends were having a jam session that night in Verona.

"They could always use another guitar player. But what they need most is a solid bass player. I've got something going on."

"What? You got a date tonight, Pip?

"Yeah, something like that."

"Hey, Steve? You play bass, don't you?"

"Well, yeah."

"You can follow a chord progression and walk a bassline, can't you? I know you can. You should go with me."

"I don't have a decent amp. It's got no balls."

"No problem, Kubacki. If you want, you can use my amp and cab. Borrow it for a week or so. It's outside in my van." Pip dropped off the cabinet and amplifier at my house a few minutes later.

I was going to a jam session with a real amp rig. An Ampeg tube head and a Fender Bassman 2 x 15 speaker cabinet. *What the fuck just happened?*

We jammed, and man, did we jam hard. I faked my way through chord progressions and walking bass lines for two and a half hours. During the session Matt looked at me when I was fucking up and pointed to the root note on his fretboard. I played triads, scales, and riffs the whole evening, faking my way through all kinds of classic rock songs.

I drank and smoked dope with adults. None of them, except Matt, knew that I was underage, and I fit in even though I was only fifteen. Must've been my full beard. The day before, I was just a nerdy small-town kid. Now, I was a musician playing out in a band. I saw how adults got along with each other. How men and women interacted. How to talk to girls. And by asking a single question, how to score with a chick. I watched Matt work his charm that night before the jam.

We had arrived first at the gig. As we waited in Matt's ride for the other musicians, a car came up and parked beside us. Matt rolled down the window and began his work. An attractive young woman opened her passenger side power window, leaned over from the driver's side, and asked if this was the right place.

Matt said, “You’ve got the right place. This is it.”

I think he was ignoring her good looks. He didn’t compliment her at all. The crucial thing was he didn’t use a cliché pick-up line. What he said to her didn’t seem to matter – it was how he talked to her. He talked to her like she was a guy. He spoke with complete confidence. Matt got out some Zig-Zags and rolled a joint while talking to the young lady. When it was ready, he held it up to the window, already knowing her answer, and asked, “Do you party?”

She did.

We smoked two joints with her before anyone else arrived, passing them back and forth between the two open car windows.

During the course of the evening, I noticed Matt doing something I had never thought of. While playing, he paid close attention to her for a few minutes and then ignored her. He kept going back and forth. Looking at her. Then looking away. He was like a yo-yo on a string. I saw the magic work and she wound up leaving the party with him.

At Matt’s car after the gig, he said, “Steve, you’re going to have to sit in back so my friend can ride up front.” He walked around to the passenger side, opened the door, tilted the seat for me to get in back, and made a gesture for his date to sit up front. Matt took me home and drove off with the young lady to be alone. Later that week, he filled me in with the details. After telling me everything he said, “Don’t say a word to Tommy about this.” I guess Tom wouldn’t understand why a married man would have a one-night stand. He’d blab to someone and it’d get back to Matt’s wife back home in Europe.

After the jam session, smoking marijuana became a regular part of my life. I wanted sex, drugs, and Rock 'n' Roll. All I needed now was sex to complete the trinity. But even after watching Matt's moves, I was having a hard time figuring it out. How was I going to get to home base when I'd only been to second base once?

That spring Gretchen broke up with me. Soon afterward someone told me Ella Dachs had a crush on me.

Ella was friends with Sophie and she started hanging out with my circle of friends. Friends of mine said Ella wasn't any good for me. One of my buddies called her *The Fish* and another one said, "Dachs has a face like a Mack truck." They were just jealous because she was interested in me. I didn't give a shit what they said. She was a well-toned volleyball player, had long legs, and perky little breasts – that's the way I like 'em – she was hot.

She showed up at my sixteenth birthday party. She was there with Sophie and some other girls and I was hanging out with my buddies. We couldn't find anyone to buy beer for us, so we grabbed several bottles of Bucka's best to drink in the woods behind my house instead. Dion, Tom, and I had some awful weed, this really crappy stuff called gack. It was all leaves and stems, not a single bud. But it was better than no weed at all. Fortunately, the girls had some decent earthy smelling Colombian buds full of shiny black seeds.

Walking through Charlene and Buckley's vegetable garden we ate some raspberries and pulled up a few baby carrots, eating them without rinsing off the dirt. We found a clearing in the woods and gathered in a circle.

Our new buddy, Franky Roberts, a senior two years ahead of us, pulled out his Camels, tapped a cigarette out of the pack and offered one to me. "Smoke?" I tried one. They were much better than Marlboro Reds. Some of the girls sat on a large fallen tree laying on the swampy ground. We passed around bottles of wine, smoked a whole bunch of pot and dozens of cigarettes.

Coming back to the house, my friends and I walked along the edge of the garden near Buckley's grapevines. The tangle of vines and leaves was full of immature green fruit. I was having a pleasant conversation with Ella as we ambled along behind the rest of the group. While everyone else went into the house Ella and I were still in the garden. I decided now was the time.

I had seen Matt work his magic at the Verona jam and I was ready to give it a try myself. He had simply asked the young woman if she partied and she said yes. But this was different, we were already partying, I couldn't ask her that. I wasn't sure what to do. If I did score, where would we go for privacy? My friends would be in the house, in the kitchen for sure, and hanging out in my bedroom too.

The tree fort of course. I stopped and turned toward her with a big smile on my face. It fell right out of my mouth.

"Wow, I'm so high. Aren't you? But you know what? I'm not too high to fuck."

She looked at me with her pellucid brown eyes, a

beaming smile on her face, leaned toward me and said, "Yeah, me too."

Trying to hide my excitement, I said, "Hey, do you want to see the tree fort? It's cool. We can go up there and talk."

"I've heard all about your fort and your special wallpaper. Frances told me all about it."

"Seriously?"

She mounted the cedar rail ladder on the main trunk and I came up behind her. As she climbed the two-by-fours attached to the upper trunk, I smelled a trail of marijuana mingling with her delightful perfume. *I wanted her. I wanted her bad.*

She pushed open the trap door and crawled onto the floor covered with mismatched carpet sample squares.

"Oh my God! It's a whole wall. Frances didn't say it was the whole wall. They're arranged so well, and I like the varnished wood. Very cool."

"It's awesome, isn't it? Dorjzaly gave those boards to me when his old man remodeled their basement."

While our friends were inside Charlene's kitchen eating God knows what, I was in the tree fort with Ella. Up in the love nest I had built from scrap wood, rusty old nails, and junk. I was going to lose my virginity. Lose my virginity *with a girl!*

We fucked so hard, I swear the whole tree shook. When we were done, we smoked a joint, a couple of cigarettes, and we had another fuck.

Afterward she said, "Oh man, that was good."

"I know. Wham bam thank you ma'am."

"You're welcome."

We joined the group for a snack in the kitchen. Bucka and Charlene didn't seem to notice we were high and drunk. If they had noticed what we were eating – whipped cream rolled inside slices of ham, Saltines with brown sugar filling, fried peanut butter and jelly sandwiches – no banana, please – they might have had a clue.

Wren walked into the kitchen, gave us a funny look and said, "What the hell are you guys eating? You're all crazy." I was surprised that our old man didn't go ballistic over her cussing. He must not have heard her.

The first time Wren swore in front of our parents, Dad went off his rocker, "I ought to wash your mouth out with soap."

I had said, "What's the big deal, Dad? I swear all the time. You tried washing my mouth out with soap once, but it didn't work. Why are you giving Wren such a hard time?"

"Young ladies shouldn't use that kind of colorful language!"

All through my sophomore year, I was still wetting the bed at night. Not as much as when I was a kid, but often enough to be a nuisance. The single bed in my basement bedroom still had a protective plastic cover enclosing the mattress. Then suddenly the bed wetting stopped. Charlene attributed the change to my growth, development, and my bones stretching out. She said I'd reached some kind milestone. Buck said with all the growing pains from elongated arms and legs, why wouldn't *his loins be bigger now too?* I had reached a milestone, for sure, and I attributed the change to getting laid. It never pissed the bed again after losing my cherry to Ella.

Dorjzaly had four tickets to go see our favorite band. One for himself and three for some of his lucky buddies. We took driver's education earlier that summer but none of us had a license yet. Carson Eachagain was into the band too and Tobi asked him to drive.

Tobi didn't know what he was in for.

Carson didn't drink and drive, but he was ready to smoke.

"Hey do you guys have any pot?"

Dion said, "Yeah. How about you, *Boogie Man*?"

"I got a couple of joints for the show. But if you guys got some for the drive, that would be awesome."

"Oh yeah we do," I said, "but it's not any good. We've got some of this shitty gack, but it's better than nothing."

"What the hell is gack?"

We got the party started, getting high and drunk as we drove down the highway to Detroit. I lit one up and Dion got one blazing – big cigar sized bombers.

Eachagain took a huge puff, choked, laughed, and said "What is this crap? It's horrible."

Dion said, "That's the gack. It makes you hack. We warned you."

"So, you call it gack?"

I said, "I call it awful. Our guy, Curly, calls it gack."

"Yeah, but it gets you high, and it's only five dollars a bag."

"That's crazy. I'd never pay that much for this crap. You guys paid five dollars a bag for this shit?"

Dion said, "Yep. But not for a sandwich bag, a big brown paper bag."

"Curly pulls huge handfuls of it out of a trash bag and stuffs a grocery bag full of it."

"Well, I guess it isn't such a bad deal then."

Tobi didn't smoke and had been quiet until then. He finally broke the silence and said, "You guys are nuts, but I don't care. Smoke 'em if you got 'em, that's what I say. The shit ought to be legal anyway."

We rode Van Dyke all the way to downtown Detroit. When we got there, we followed the attendant's orders as he directed us into the parking ramp.

At the front of Joe Louis Arena, we had to climb a massive staircase, it was three or four stories high and must've been a hundred yards wide. It's the biggest flight of stairs this country boy has ever seen. As soon as we got to our seats, Carson lit up one of his good doobies before the start of the show. We smoked another one of his joints about an hour into the performance. The show was amazing.

After the concert, we walked across the pedestrian bridge to the car ramp. I had a strange feeling as we walked through the bridge. It felt like we were inside an enormous Habitrail hamster tube. We walked through the huge pipe, climbed several flights of stairs, and with Tobi's help – the only sober one – managed to find Carson's car in the mind-boggling parking structure.

Traffic was bumper to bumper as we left the garage. Eachagain asked how we should get out of there. I had no idea how to get home because I was high as hell, and Dion, also totally fried, didn't know either. Tobi suggested one way but Carson had already made up his mind and turned in the opposite direction.

We were driving along Jefferson Avenue and seemed to be going north. But soon we entered a gritty manufacturing district where Jefferson turns into Rosa Parks Boulevard. Back then none of us had heard of Rosa Parks. The only black person we gave a shit about was Jimi Hendrix. *Who the fuck is Rosa Parks?* All I knew was *we were going the wrong way.*

I wanted to get the hell out of there. My buddies were looking around the neighborhood and I could tell none of them felt safe either. We were out of place, very out of place, in a very black neighborhood. I felt how a black person probably felt, with so damn many white people, in Huron County.

Carson's hands and elbows started shaking and a mild sweat appeared on his forehead. He turned off Rosa Parks. Lost, panicky, and driving too fast on badly potholed streets, he sped into an unlit section of the next block. Going even faster, he went up a small hill and crossed some railroad tracks. The bottom of his car crunched as the rocker panels dragged over the tracks. We came down the other side of the slight hill and the red dashboard light came on, *yeah that red light,* and the engine belched out a horrific grinding noise.

He yelled, "Holy shit! We're fucked!"

A huge streak of black oil poured onto the street behind us.

Tobi said, "Carson, we've got to get off the road." Then he yelled, "Now! Right, fucking, now!"

"Where, Tobi? Where?"

"Right here, man."

He pulled into the lot of an abandoned factory. Saccharin steam and foul smoke spewed up from under the hood. *Now what?* Dion said there was a pay phone near a White Castle we had passed a few blocks back. We got out of the wrecked car and walked toward the restaurant. The phone was in working order despite its heavily graffitied and dilapidated appearance. None of us had any change. It didn't matter anyway. Who the hell could we call in Detroit at one in the morning?

A haggard old black man walked up to us and said, "One of you boys got a light?" as he leaned towards us with his cigar. He had a broad, friendly smile on his face.

Dion whipped out a lighter. "Sure do, man."

Roll-click-spark.

He leaned toward the flame for a moment and then pulled back. "Hah! I was kidding you boys. This ain't no damn cigar, it's a *tied stick.*"

We had heard of the legendary Thai-stick. Thoughtfully manicured buds carefully tied to a shish kebab skewer. And this is where we first stumbled into it. In the middle of a rough neighborhood at Fort and Livernois, down the street from a disintegrating Fisher Body Plant. The old dude tried to sell us some of the shit. I was ready to purchase, and could tell by the look on their faces, Carson and Dion wanted to buy some too.

Tobi said, "No way, man. No, sir. What we need is a tow truck. Are there any garages nearby?"

"There ain't no garages around here, just more of

these assembly plants." He nodded, wished us luck, and returned to the picnic table, his buddies, and a stack of greasy hamburgers smothered with minced onions.

"Hey guys, my Aunt Lily and Uncle Marc live in Detroit. Maybe we can call them for help."

"Where Kubacki? I need to get my car out of here now."

"Warren."

"I thought you said they lived in Detroit?"

Dion said, "Close enough, Carson. Close enough."

Tobi said, "That's about forty minutes from here."

We interrupted the old men eating hamburgers and asked them for change. None of them had any change. At least that's what they said. Why would they want to help out a bunch of lost and marooned white boys anyway?

I picked up the phone, dialed zero, and asked for information. The operator patched me through. Information looked up the number and dialed it for me. The operator came back on and asked for two-twenty-five for two minutes.

"I'd like to place the call collect."

The phone rang several times when the operator said, "No one's answering."

"Can you let it ring a few more times?"

After several more rings, my Aunt Lily answered the phone. I told her, it's Steve, we were at a concert at The Joe, got lost, and my buddy's car broke down. We're stranded. When I told her where we were, she had no idea where the hell it was. She handed the phone to Uncle Marcus.

My uncle had worked for decades as foreman in a factory downtown and he didn't know where the hell we were. He had to get out a road map to find us. I could hear him unfolding the map. It took a minute for him to find the right intersection. He said, "I'll be there as soon as I can," and hung up.

About an hour and a half later, he rolled up Fort Street, turned into the White Castle parking lot, and stopped next to the phone booth. He said hello to Thai-stick-man and his friends and they chatted for a few minutes. Uncle Marc is a real people person, and having worked with many different kinds of folks, could strike up a conversation with anyone.

My friends and I piled into my uncle's big yellow Lincoln and headed to Warren. He drove us through a labyrinth of city side streets and expressways, criss-crossed through the narrow, swanky streets of Zajac's neighborhood, and finally pulled into his driveway.

Inside the house, Aunt Lily was making breakfast for Marc and the hungry boys she was expecting. Uncle Marc had enough time to hit the shower, get ready for work, and have a quick bite to eat. My buddies and I said thank you as he ran out the door.

Later that morning, Carson hired a wrecker to tow his car from downtown to Warren. The oil pan had been torn completely off. Fortunately, Tobi had told Eachagain to get off the road before the engine blew up. The tow truck arrived at the house early in the afternoon, and a couple hours later, when Uncle Marc got home from work, he drove Eachagain and Tobi to the parts store. When they returned, Marc gave my buddies a tour of his garage, unlocked his tool chest, and left them to make repairs. Eachagain wasn't much of a mechanic, but Tobi knew his way around an automobile.

Each of us had called our parents the night before. We called them again that afternoon to tell them what was going on and that we were all right. When I talked to Charlene, she said she was with my girlfriends, Ella, Sophie, and Gretchen. They were at the house helping Charlie hull peas from the garden. I tried to imagine them and my mom sitting on an old quilt, shelling peas. *Why was my old girlfriend, Gretchen, hanging out with Ella?*

While Carson and Tobi made the repairs to the car, Dion and I listened to the WRIF and WLLZ and watched music videos on MTV. We came outside once in a while to see how our buddies were doing in the garage. After checking their progress, we took walks around the neighborhood. We found a new construction site and smoked some of the gack in a rough framed house.

Seeing the framework of a building as it goes up has always fascinated me. It's like being inside a large animal's skeleton, inside the rib cage, watching the flesh appear. As a kid, my old man and I had often gone into building sites to check it out.

Dion and I came back from *one of our walks* to find Eachagain and Dorjzaly had finished the repairs. We made a long-winded Michigan goodbye to Marc and Lily, the usual twenty minutes, and drove back to Bad Axe.

The car ran great!

As soon as we got back in town, I called Ella to set up a date. I was going to meet her at the house where she was babysitting. We did this fairly often because I couldn't always borrow the Cordoba and it was a good arrangement for a couple of hot-to-trot teenagers. She sent the kids to bed and moments later we were going at it. We wound up in the bathroom, her perched up on the edge of the vanity, and me banging away.

Before dating me, Ella had dated a guy in his late twenties and had probably learned lots of moves from him. I was the happy beneficiary of Ella's experience. I didn't have to make much effort to please her. *She knew how to take care of herself.*

Later that month, Ella and I went to the county fair.

"I've always wanted to go on the Zipper. Have you ever ridden it?"

She said, "No. That ride is always breaking down and someone gets stuck spinning around at the top. Sometimes the cars fall off track and come crashing to the ground. People get killed on that thing."

"I know it's dangerous and people puke on it all the time. But I've never been on it. I want to try it. Come on."

"No way. Not me."

We continued down the fairway to play some games.

While I played, entranced by the game, ignoring her and shooting a strong steady stream of water into a plastic clown's face, a loud buzzer suddenly went off. Some young kid won the stuffed animal.

Ella was gone. *Where the hell did she go?* I figured she took off with one of her friends but didn't see her anywhere nearby. I walked to the Zipper to watch it whirl and twirl around. As I was staring at it, two girls on Ella's volleyball team came up and said hi.

Cailyn said, "You want to try it, Steve? I have twelve tickets."

"Let's do it."

The other girl said, "Aren't you here with Dachs?"

"She won't mind if we go for a ride."

"Nah, she won't give a shit."

Of course, she did give a shit. In fact, she was pissed off. I didn't get it. *She's my girlfriend, not my wife. What's the big deal?*

At the end of fair week, Carson and Sophie had a house party. Everybody brought their own beer, Mrs. Eachagain had some in the fridge, several of my friends and myself had pot. We had five kinds of good weed, none of it was that shitty gack.

It was a hot and humid night, and with a strong buzz going, I didn't need much encouragement when Ella suggested we take a shower in the upstairs bathroom. After we finished our wet romp, we bumped into Argent and Gretchen making out at the top of the stairs. They stopped as soon as they saw us. I had just ripped a piece with Ella and didn't care what Gretchen and Tommy were doing.

"You can have her if you'd like, Tommy. You guys should take a shower. Did you see Mrs. Eachagain's sign on the bathroom wall? It says, *Conserve water, take a shower with a friend.*"

After the party, I didn't have any smoke left and

needed another bag. I had to get money fast but there was no grass to cut. Grandma's yard was a dust bowl. The lawn wasn't growing at all. Not even any tall weeds to knock down. I had already cleaned her house before the fair and that money was gone. But I figured my buddy, Rizzo, and I could pull another scam.

I had become good at shoplifting. Pocketknives and trinkets weren't worth the trouble anymore. Now I stole big ticket items. Lots of tools, small expensive tools, and Hendricks returned them for cash.

Rizzo and I went into the store and looked around for something to cover the cost of a half-ounce or ounce of weed. Once we spotted something, he went outside and waited in the car. I made sure no customers or clerks were around, concealed the tool in my pants or jacket, and took it out to the car. Rizzo went back in the store and made the return to get the cash.

The cashiers got to know Hendricks and stopped letting him return items without a receipt. We started asking our buddies to do it. We rotated between our friends to make the returns. We asked Luke, Derrick, Boyd, Stosh, Dion, Tommy or any other convenient stoner to do the dirty work. They were happy to help, because once they got the cash, we took off to see our pot dealer.

He lived twenty miles away in Harbor Beach. Mr. Green Jeans kept his pot in the top drawer of his bedroom dresser, pre-weighed, and sorted by size. We gave him the money, he gave us the bag, and then we smoked some pot with him. We rolled one out of our bag and he rolled one or two from his stash under the couch.

After hooking up, my friends and I gallivanted around for hours. I drove my Ford Fiesta down backroads or along the shoreline of Lake Huron and Saginaw Bay with my accomplices on a pot smoking, burrito eating, Mountain Dew guzzling road cruise. If we had spent all our money on weed and couldn't put gas in my car for a road cruise we went to Rizzo's mom's.

He lived at her tiny two-bedroom apartment where he didn't have a proper bedroom. The kid slept on a cot-sized mattress in his mom's walk-in closet. We crammed in there and made a thick cloud of smoke in her closet. Mrs. Hendricks's clothes, closet, and the rest of her bedroom always reeked of pot and cigarettes.

At the beginning of sophomore year, I was taking college prep classes, but usually finished my work at school to have time to party with friends in the evening.

The evening's the great time, isn't it, boy?

Between partying with my pals and trying to spend time with Ella I was getting pulled in two different directions. Ella wanted me to spend my free time with her and I wanted to spend my free time getting stoned with my buddies. I felt as if she was controlling me. I felt trapped. I liked getting laid whenever I wanted, but wasn't that into her, and still had feelings for Gretchen. I thought of giving up on Ella. I wanted to party whenever I wanted, wanted to chase after Gretchen again. Despite the great sex, I broke it off and dumped Ella.

Within a couple weeks Gretchen came back. I had been playing games with her and she had been playing games with me. She had been hanging out with Ella like they were bosom buddies. The incident at Eachagain's party – poor Tommy – all Argent got out of it was frustration. I had played it cool, pretending I didn't care about Gretchen and Tommy making out. Pretending I didn't give a shit when I really wanted her back. I did get her back and everything was going my way.

The Maddoxes parked a small camper trailer in their driveway. It had electricity, a space heater, and was ready to sleep in year-round. Someone in Gretchen's family was always sleeping out in it. Wasn't long before I was sleeping in it too, and getting some action.

I had crawled out of my bedroom window before, but now there was a girl at stake, there was no way I was going to get caught. I had to be careful to make it a regular thing. When no one was home, I removed the tilting glass frame and outer screen from my bedroom window. I oiled the squeaky hinges on the window and installed inconspicuous handles on the inside and outside of the screen. Now, I could sneak out whenever I wanted, sleep over at Gretchen's, and try to get laid.

With Gretchen, it wasn't sex on demand like with Ella, who wanted it as bad as me. Gretchen wasn't as sexual as her. Something seemed to be blocking Gretchen's impulses. When she had the urge, it was strong, but there was something going on. She didn't enjoy herself and didn't always want to have sex.

One time, I was suffering from a bad case of blue balls and did a crude thing trying to have my way with her.

Sophie was sleeping over at Gretchen's. The girls asked me to come over and see them. *Did both of them want it?* No. They just wanted to get high. I smoked a couple of my doobies with them, we talked for a while, and eventually Sophie fell asleep.

That was my opportunity. I made moves on Gretchen. Kissing her, groping her waist and breasts, but she wasn't having any of it.

"Not now. Sophie might wake up."

Gretchen was definitely not in the mood and I couldn't understand why. We could be quiet. She didn't make much noise anyway. I kept trying to persuade her but she wouldn't budge. I was mad with her and said, "I might as well stick my dick in this shoe," as I picked up her loafer, "than bother with you."

The next day at school, Gretchen and Sophie gave me hell. Sophie said, "You're such an asshole, Steve. I was awake the whole time."

The first time I broke into the junior high it was for the hell of it. I wanted to see the hallways and class rooms at night and check out parts of the basement I'd never seen before.

One day at school, I had noticed the windows in the stairwell landings were not locked. The locks were old, covered in decades of paint, and some were broken or missing. A convenient flat roof was under the windows of the east stair landing. It would be easy to climb up the sturdy downspout to the roof, crawl through a window, and step onto the landing. The old Quonset hut next to the school would block the view from the street. It looked so easy.

The second time I broke in I had a more malicious plan. I wanted to steal Ventdebois's strobotuner for our garage band. Argent, Dion, and I didn't have a tuner, and when we tuned by ear, our music sounded off. So, I did it, I broke into the school a second time, but this time I stole the tuner, a pair of handheld crash cymbals, and a handful of drum mallets and sticks. We needed that shit. Now Dion and Argent would have plenty of options when they took turns on the drum kit.

Frances Sawicki and her girlfriend couldn't believe I had broken in to the school. They thought I had stolen the gear during the day. How the hell could I walk out with a tuner, a giant pair of crash cymbals, and a bunch of drum sticks in the daytime? I had to break in a third time to prove it to the girls. I took them with me to show them how it was done.

Bucka liked to read the local newspaper while sitting on the commode. When I was a young kid, I walked in there all the time while he was taking a shit. I sat on the edge of the bathtub talking with the old man, and every now and then, he'd look at me over the top of his Huron Daily Tribune to chit chat.

The old man was probably in the john when he read the story headlined, BAND EQUIPMENT STOLEN FROM BAD AXE JUNIOR HIGH. The article said to contact the Bad Axe Police; Mr. Fairfield, principal; or Mr. Ventdebois, band director, if you have any information. Buckley and Charlene often talked about the news and local gossip and Mom put the pieces together when Dad had told her about the break in. She checked out our rehearsal space to confirm her suspicions. Charlie called the police and told them about the *new* music gear that had shown up in her garage.

The police made as many charges against me as they could. Breaking and entering, petty larceny, trespassing, and they even threw in a curfew violation. I avoided jail time by agreeing to the judge's conditions. He tabled my case and said if I stayed out of trouble for ninety days the whole thing would be dismissed. The judge realized how messed up I was and made me visit a psychiatrist. I met with the shrink once a week.

After that, to fit the part, I started dressing in better clothes. Trendy, fashionable outfits – skin tight parachute pants, brightly colored shirts with funky geometric patterns, and thin leather ties – instead of tattered blue jeans and concert t-shirts.

The head shrinker was interested in how I got money to buy beer and marijuana, keep gas in my car, and yet, didn't have a regular job. I told him the money came from doing work for Grandma. He didn't believe me. Can you blame him? So, I told him a half-truth and that seemed to satisfy him.

I said I fronted bags of pot from my dealer, smoked some of it, and sold the rest to my friends to pay back my weed guy.

The main source of money was really from shoplifting scams. I didn't tell him how I stole tools and stereo equipment and returned the schwag for cash. Why the hell would I do that? I didn't trust this guy or the whole doctor patient confidentiality thing.

But I did tell him about driving drunk and driving high. I even told him about the time Rizzo and I smoked a bunch of dope, ate some purple micro dots, and my car felt like it was shooting through a pneumatic tube at a drive-through bank as we barreled down the road between the enormous snow drifts on the shoulder.

By this time my friends and I were using dots, a small pill supposedly made of mescaline, but was actually LSD. We also dropped blotter acid and ate psilocybin mushrooms. And if it was around, we couldn't resist sweet, floral, pain-relieving opium, which is really a crude black tar heroin. Sometimes, to stay awake and party through the night and some of the next day, we used cocaine. Sometimes we snorted biker's coke, also known as crystal tea, which I am now sure was actually methamphetamine speed. My friends and I tried whatever came our way. Marijuana was my drug of choice but we tried anything we could get our hands on. It turns out, marijuana was my gateway drug *or maybe it was the Karo syrup.*

I also told my doctor about the time Hendricks and I were parked on a back road in the middle of nowhere. It was during a bad snow storm. Hendricks was rolling a joint on the rubber floor mat of Dad's Chevy S-10.

"Kubacki, did you see that bud move? I swear to fucking God it jumped!"

"Yeah, I saw it too. It fucking jumped!"

"The fucking thing looks alive."

"I know, it looks like a goddamn grasshopper!"

The shrink looked at me with a serious look on his face.

"I must tell you, it's my policy that if you show up for an appointment intoxicated your session will be canceled."

The dumbass gave me a way to avoid my therapy

session whenever I didn't want to go. All I had to do was show up drunk or high or both.

Gretchen and I were fumbling along trying to make something out of our romance. We had a lot of things in common – same taste in music, wearing good clothes, and acting out the angst of moody teenagers. She wrote things like, *Life privilege or punishment?* on her folders where a lot of girls doodled hearts and scribbled a boy's names or initials. She was deep, deep and dark like me, but we didn't have an animal connection. When we did connect it was amazing, at least for me, but she only stared at the ceiling. It always seemed she was somewhere else when we were together.

Gretchen, a bunch of our friends, and I were in the park one afternoon, hanging out, smoking pot, measuring a summer's day. I started an argument with her in front of everyone. She hadn't put out in a while and I couldn't shut up about it. I got hot headed. Didn't know how to stop myself and did something I never imagined I would do.

I had never been in a fight at school. I avoided fights by running away like a chicken. I was angry with Gretchen. Boiling over with steam. Getting physical with a woman has only ever happened that one time because I felt so terrible about it. But the pressure had built up and my hostility came out through my body. The negative energy bolted down my leg and I kicked her. It was more of a push, but I pushed her with my foot. I kicked her squarely on the ass. The sole of my shoe left a dark muddy stain on the bottom of her white cotton shorts. I attacked her out of anger. I ruined her pants. I ruined her. I ruined myself. *What the fuck did I do?*

Shortly after the scene, the Maddoxes moved to a bigger house on the edge of town. Their new home was in the same subdivision where Bucka's boss, Mr. Paigne, lived. About a month after the move, Gretchen broke up with me, again, and started dating her new neighbor, Mitch Paigne. I can't blame him. A cute girl had moved into his neighborhood and she was available.

I couldn't handle it and started chasing them through town when they were on dates. Mitch would turn around and chase me to even the score. It was ridiculous. At the end of the school year, they attended senior prom together. I knew they were going and wanted to take a date of my own to make her jealous. Luckily, a girl asked me out to the dance. I had no interest in her, told her I would go, and I made it clear we would be going as friends. Just friends.

My date and I showed up at the Verona Hills Golf Course. As we walked from her car to the clubhouse, Paigne and Gretchen came tearing out of the parking lot in his custom 4 x 4 truck. The fucker squealed his tires, honked the horn, and waved at us as they flew out of the lot. With a smirk on my face, I waved back and resisted the urge to flip him the bird.

We sneaked in a pint of booze, got drunk behind the club house, and smoked a joint on the first hole tee. Hung out for a while and checked out what people were wearing. Two girls had worn identical dresses and one of them bawled about it. After finishing our bottle and smoking the rest of the dope, we left, and she drove me home.

Later that summer, Buckley and Charlene rented a house for a week. It was a cute cottage on Saginaw Bay next to the public beach in Caseville. Before the vacation, Gretchen had broken up with Mitch and started dating me again. While I was spending time with my family, Gretchen was camping with her church group at Sleeper State Park five miles away.

I couldn't stand being away from her for a whole week. Since she couldn't leave camp, I decided to go see her. I needed my visit to look innocent and asked Wren and her friend, Leigh, to go with me. While there, I could get her alone, away from her goody-goody bible-thumping friends. I planned to have my way with her in a sandy clearing in the woods. But Gretchen wasn't feeling it that day, and since she didn't like public displays of affection, she wouldn't even give me a kiss. I told her, in front of all her friends, about my blue balls.

She said she had to go, went with the group to load onto the bus, and they headed back to the cabins. I couldn't let her go and followed in my car. I sped up to the bus, swerved into the passing lane, and drove beside the bus under Gretchen's open window.

Sitting beside me, Wren yelled, "What the hell are you doing, Stephen Mark?"

I didn't pass, but stayed next to the bus. I honked the horn and backfired the engine several times. A car was coming down the road, so I slowed down to get behind the bus. The car drove by and I sped up to ride beside the bus again. After backfiring the engine a few more times, I downshifted into third, squawked the tires, passed the bus, and flew down the road as it turned into the camp site.

Wren told me to pull the car over. Her and Leigh got out and said they would walk back to Caseville.

That evening, the Huron County Sheriff and Caseville Police showed up at the vacation house. I had been bragging to Gretchen and her friends and told them our cottage was on a street *named after me.* The county cops issued a citation for reckless driving and an equipment violation for loud exhaust. One of the cops said they had told Gretchen how to file a restraining order. I knew she wouldn't file one, and even if she did, no one could keep me away from my woman *with a piece of paper.*

Charlie and Bucka didn't say much about the cops showing up. They were probably sick and tired of my bullshit. I realize now, they had tried reaching out to me many times, they definitely had. But they hadn't tried hard enough. I think they simply wanted to enjoy their vacation despite me wrecking my own.

That evening they took the rest of the family out to dinner. While they were away, Dion, Sophia, Roberts, and my new buddy, Carl Hutte, stopped by to party. We drank a fifth of Jack Daniels and twenty or thirty beers. We sat by a small bonfire, talking, drinking, and smoking pot.

Buckley and Charlene came down to the beach after dinner to say hi to everyone. After a few minutes of chit-chat, they went inside to go to bed. When the whiskey was finished, we wrote a strange note, put it in the empty bottle, and threw it into Saginaw Bay.

My friends left to go home.

Before passing out on the couch, I staggered behind the row of cottages and crept along the hedges down to the M-25. I climbed up the galvanized steel pole at the end of our lane and tore off the sign which said *Stephens Drive – Private* and took it home as a souvenir.

Ten

Sometimes hanging-out at Rudd's house, I would see a skinny, long-legged girl walking up and down the sidewalks on Luke's block. She had curly, spiked-up hair, lacquered with a ton of hairspray. Almost every time I was at his place, I saw the leggy chick walking from her grandma's house, around the corner, and up the street to her uncle's place a few houses away from Rudd's.

"She's got a body that just won't stop."

"I know it, Luke. Madge is so hot."

Hutte, Luke, and I were smoking pot one sunny afternoon in the Verona Cemetery. I was sitting in the passenger seat rolling a joint when two girls on horseback came cantering down Roller Coaster Road. They reached the bottom of the hill, came into the cemetery, and trotted to our car.

It was that hot chick I kept seeing in Rudd's neighborhood, Madge Fleeting, and her girlfriend, Bonita, was with her. If the horses weren't enough of a clue, you could tell by the way they dressed that these girls had rich daddies. Madge's old man owned a Centennial Farm where he grew cash crops, raised cattle, and kept horses. Bonita's dad owned factories in Bad Axe and Ubly. The girls lived about two miles down the road from the cemetery.

I couldn't believe it, but there she was, Madge, riding on horseback, in full English dressage attire, talking to us, *talking to me.*

Madge showed up in my computer class that fall at the start of my senior year. About thirty kids met off campus at the learning center in Bad Axe. Students from Huron County, Sanilac County, and Tuscola County drove to the HISD building for the class. Madge and four other girls from Ubly were in the class, and all of them were cute. I was still dating Gretchen but I was looking for more action.

Early in the semester Tobias pulled me aside and said, "Hey Kubacki, Fleeting's got the hots for you. She wants your dick!"

"Are you kidding me? Madge is interested in me?"

She must have realized I was clueless to her flirting and had asked Tobi to say something. Things moved fast after that.

Soon afterward, Stosh Zajac and I were carousing around in my Fiesta on Friday night. Fleeting saw Zee and I and flagged us down. She was cruising around the endless loop of Bad Axe with Bonita and another girl. I pulled over and we chatted with the girls. They wanted to go cruising with us. My car was too tiny, so Stosh and I got out of my car and went with them.

Madge told Zee he could drive. Her two girlfriends sat up front with him, and Madge and I climbed into the back seat. Stosh turned around in the trailer park where Huttes lived and we took off. Minutes into the cruise, I start making out with her. She pressed her face into mine and twirled her tongue in my mouth. After that I don't know where the hell we went. I'm not sure because we were seriously preoccupied. Madge and I were lost inside each other's face. Zee looked in the rear-view mirror every few minutes to see if we were still breathing. Her friends tried their best to ignore our lip smacking but their giggles gave them away. They couldn't ignore us. Her car was fast, she was fast, and she wasn't shy.

The music and the car ignition went off. We looked up and realized Stosh had parked the car. Our friends were craning their necks over the front seat watching us go at it. The spell was broken.

We said goodnight to the ladies, the girls went back to Ubly, and Zee and I made another loop through town before going home.

Madge and I went out alone on our next date. I picked her up, drove down her road, crossed Wadsworth Road, and continued on Roller Coaster Road into the valley of Willow Creek's headwater. The next mile is all hills and I drove her through the hills the proper way. I sped up a hill, hugged the shoulder in case someone was coming towards us, let off the gas at the top of the hill – sending our stomachs into our throats – and coasted down the other side. I did it again on the next hill, and the next, all the way through the mile. I turned right at the cemetery, drove another mile, and went across Verona Road into the dead-end. At the road's end, I kept driving into the field of tall grass and wildflowers. I parked the car and put on some good music.

We necked for a while and a few minutes later we took off all our clothes. She knew how to fuck better than anyone else. She fucked me harder than I'd ever been fucked before. She was crazy. I felt the raw power of her sexual energy. She let loose, pounding into me, and I pounded back into her.

After that first night, we went on dates four or five times a week. She was insatiable and I couldn't get enough of her. Got so worked up on a date I would go home and masturbate to porno mags. Why not? Cyndi Lauper was always doing the *She Bop.*

After getting in trouble for the break in, I had changed my image and was dressing so well that some tough guys at school started to tease me. They said things like, "You're such a wuss!" or, "You goddamned faggot!" They threatened to beat me up because I looked so good. I dressed much better than they did in their shit-kicker boots, jeans, and plaid flannel shirts. *Only a homosexual could dress that well, so I must be one.*

Older and bigger than me, I'm sure they could have easily kicked my ass, but I kept them away by pouring my derision upon anything they did. "Go ahead and beat me up. You'd look pretty tough beating up a faggot. You fucking assholes!" I didn't give a fuck what they thought of me or what they could do to me.

Senior year was great. I had two girlfriends, Gretchen and Madge, a work study job, and since I'd taken a lot of classes in my first three years, had two study hall sessions in the morning. I didn't study much, rarely had homework, and used the time to read a book or put my head down on the table and take a nap.

Lifting my head one foggy morning, I saw a girl I hadn't noticed before. *She must be a freshman.* A new seating arrangement had put her directly across from me. How could I have not noticed her before? She was sitting in her chair, reading, taking notes, and looking my way every now and then. This girl wasn't shy, and for once, I was not oblivious to her behavior. How could I miss it? She had short wavy hair, wore a fuzzy blue sweater with a pretty white beaded necklace, and was staring at me as she fondled her No. 2 pencil and nibbled the lucky pink eraser tip. I knew she wanted me but I didn't have any idea who she was.

At lunch, I saw her talking to Hutte's sister, Natalie. Looking in my direction, the girls whispered to each other, and started giggling. Natalie got up from her chair and headed for the hallway. I set down my soybean hamburger on the divided plastic plate and went after Natalie to ask about the girl in the blue sweater.

The girl from study hall, Maisie Pearl, thought I was cute. The girls wanted to meet at my house, talk, and see my bedroom.

They showed up and knocked on the back door.

I yelled, "Come on in," from the bottom of the stairs and Maisie and Natalie came down to my room.

The three of us sat on the bed. Natalie said my posters and other stuff hanging on the walls was cool. Miss Pearl wasn't interested in the décor.

She didn't say much, skipped the small talk, grabbed my neck, and pulled me to her face. She pressed her lips to mine, forced my mouth open, bit at my tongue, and licked my teeth. It felt as if she was trying to crawl inside my mouth. I licked and bit back at her. Natalie watched with her eyes wide open as Maisie and I made out and pawed at each other. The heat was building up between us and I wanted to take things further but Natalie was sitting there watching us. We kept at it for twenty or thirty minutes before we stopped.

Natalie looked at us with young lust in her eyes and said, "Oh my God! I've never seen anything like that before. You guys are so hot."

She wasn't alone. I'd never seen anything like that either. Maisie had shown me how to kiss in unimaginable ways. I needed to have some time alone with this young chick. We set up a date for Saturday afternoon.

"Pick me up tomorrow, but don't come to my house. Meet me about halfway down the road. There's a ditch at the bottom of the hill. I'll be waiting there for you."

Driving over the small hill, I expected to see her at the side of the gravel road but she wasn't there. I rolled past the ditch and stopped when I saw her scrambling up the bank to the road. Maisie got in the car. Her perfume ensconced me as we embraced. We smashed our lips together in a sloppy wet French kiss.

When we let go, she said in a soft, airy voice, "Hi Steve."

I said, "Hi Maisie," as if in a dream.

I turned right at the next intersection, drove across Ubly Road, and headed into Verona Hills. I drove past the Willow Creek swamp, ignored the cable across the driveway, and barreled through the ditch into the abandoned gravel quarry. I parked the car on a hillside next to the pit, well out of sight from the road. We kissed for several minutes while listening to music.

I pulled off her white tennis shoes and her floral-patterned blue jeans. I was down on the floor, lapping her muff when she asked, "What is this weird music?"

"Why? Do you like it? It's good, isn't it?"

She didn't answer.

We switched places.

I took off my Levi's, sat in the reclined seat, and she got down on the floor. She gave me an amazing blowjob. No one had ever done that for me before. Not even the boys on my block. She knew exactly what I wanted. Exactly what I needed. How in the hell did such a young girl know her way around like that? She took her time, nearly half an hour, to finish her blessed work. When she was done, I was completely satisfied, exhausted, and regrettably, didn't take things any further. I was a little bit scared because she was so young.

We got dressed.

I don't remember taking her home, or for that matter, how I got home. I wasn't even stoned or drunk. I had to wear high collared shirts for several days to hide the hickies around my neck. I didn't want Gretchen or Madge to notice. They must have seen the necklace of bruises, but I don't think it mattered to them. It made them more competitive.

Later that week, I had dropped Gretchen of at home and was driving around town. I saw Madge cruising around with Bonita. I followed them into the McDonald's parking lot. The girls had gone to the bathroom and I waited for them in a booth. They took their time, preoccupied with touching up their hair, make-up, and for sure, Madge over spraying the seductively toxic perfume she wore. The girls finally came out and we talked for a few minutes.

I gave Madge a juicy kiss and said, "I'll see you in class tomorrow." I went outside, climbed into my car, and sped away.

On the way home, I saw my favorite cop, Officer

Brighid. He had pulled over, Buddy, one of my classmates. To get a closer look, I turned down the side street. Brighid had taken several beer bottles from Bud's vehicle and put them on the roof of his car. *What the fuck? That ain't right!* So, in spite of the cop, I screamed out the passenger window, "Fuck you, Brick-head!" and backfired my engine while driving by the traffic stop.

That fucker was always harassing me and my buddies. He's the reason I got all those traffic tickets. I can't tell you how many tickets I got from that cop. I eventually lost my driver's license for six months because of him.

Brick-head left the scene, let my drunk friend drive home, and chased after me. He followed me through the neighborhood. He didn't turn on his red and blue strobe lights or the siren. He was right on my ass, it was obvious he was following, but he didn't give any signal to pull over. Not a pointed finger or even a wave of his chubby hand. I kept on driving. I drove slowly, carefully, legally, used my turn signals, and finally turned into Argent's driveway. I ignored the cop like he wasn't following me and walked across the lawn to the front door.

As Izzy was opening the door to let me in, a blur of dark blue flew out of the vehicle and onto the porch. Brighid grabbed my wrists and locked me in handcuffs so quickly I didn't know what was happening. He tightened the steel bracelets, led me to the cruiser, carefully cradled the back of my head, and shoved me in back. The seat was made of hard black plastic. *What the fuck's up with that?* A clear acrylic barrier separated the back seat from the driver compartment. There weren't any handles or locks on the doors.

He took me to the county jail, booked me, finger printed me, and placed me in a holding cell. I demanded my free phone call because they hadn't offered one. The turnkey groaned, let me out of the cage, and gave me two dimes.

"The phones over there, kid."

Click-click-click-click-clack.

Dad came to pick me up. He didn't have to post bail. I had enough of my own cash. The old man was disappointed, quite disgusted with the situation, couldn't look at me on the way home, and said nothing.

Even though I wasn't properly mirandized, the Bad Axe district attorney said the arrest was legal. The DA charged me with fleeing and eluding despite no indication from the cop to pull over. But with help from a pro bono attorney, a friend of the family, the charge was reduced to disobeying an officer. Because I had mouthed off to a cop the charge stuck. A charge which was a minor misdemeanor back then, but now, decades later is considered a felony.

I spent the rest of that fall, and part of the winter, dating three girls. I worked a crazy three girl rotation. It was silly how much action I was getting. I was a real man now – yet I was sick, *mentally sick,* but I didn't know it.

What I did know was fatigue. I was sick and tired

of being tired. Sometimes I had two of them in one day. They were wearing me out. I started to think maybe I should pick one. Just one. The best one. All three of my girls were smart, sexy, funny, and beautiful. It would be tough, but I had to choose my favorite.

Maisie had asked me to come to where she was babysitting. I parked my car down the road and walked through a snow-covered field into the back yard. I trudged around to the front porch, saw her through the living room window, and waved. She ran to the front door and let me into the house.

The kids were in bed and we immediately got busy. We smashed our faces together, trying to asphyxiate one another. We tore off each other's jeans and threw them on the floor. I had made up my mind, I was going to fuck Maisie this time, but I wasn't in a rush. She was the only girl who would suck it, so I let her. She was working her mouth magic when someone pulled into the driveway.

The parents were home early from their date! *What the fuck!*

She said, "You've got to get out of here," as she handed me my pants. I tried to put them on as she grabbed my coat and shoes. "You've got to get out of here now! Use the back door and get out of here as fast as you can." My date was ruined, but had other things on my mind, I didn't want to get caught or Maisie to get in trouble.

Outside it was snowing, drifting, and cold as hell. Running through the field with my coat unzipped, my shoes in one hand and trying to button my pants with the other, I stumbled and fell in the snow. I made it to the car and was lacing up my shoes when the parents' car backed out of the driveway. The vehicle turned onto the gravel road toward me. *Maisie's house is the other way.* What the hell? I was screwed! The car rolled up closer and I realized it was not the parents' car. It was my buddy, Dion. The passenger window rolled down and Dion, Stosh, and Argent hooted, hollered, and laughed at me.

"You're a bunch of assholes! What the fuck are you guys doing out here?"

Dion said, "We wanted to see how your date was going. We're going to a party in Ubly. You want to go?"

"You guys ruined my fucking date. Did you see me running half naked through the field?"

"Yeah," Stosh said, "we saw you. It was hilarious."

"I hate you guys. So, where is this party anyway?"

I got in my car, raced past them, back fired my engine as I passed, and beat them to the party.

At the party, I was wondering why the hell I didn't go back to the house and fuck Maisie. The parents weren't there and she had probably figured out it was my buddies goofing around with me. What the hell was I thinking? I screwed up, I screwed up bad. I should have went back.

Maisie was the wildest of the three girls, but I had made a terrible decision by not going back to her when my buddies interrupted us. She must've been pissed, but I didn't know, we hadn't talked since it happened. I wanted to have sex with her, keep seeing her, but what would happen in June? At seventeen I was still a minor, but what kind of trouble would I face for dating a fourteen-year-old girl when I turned eighteen in June? *Jailbait for sure.* Besides, I didn't know how to relate to her, kept avoiding her at school, and didn't talk to her anymore.

Madge was hypersexual but she was also wrapped up in building networks, stock portfolios, and her resumé. I didn't give a crap about any of that stuff. I broke things off by writing her a note. Scribbled something on a scrap of paper about our relationship being nothing but young lust and gave it to her in computer lab. She cried in class. When she stopped bawling, she walked up to me and said I was an asshole and my car was a little tin can. After confronting me, she smacked her keyboard a few times, slammed her chair into a desk, ran out of class, and hid in the bathroom.

Gretchen was the least sexual, she was always holding back. But she was also the most creative and we connected on a dark emotional level. She had secrets like I had secrets. In the end, I chose her, and dated only her. *She was the one.*

A few days after my eighteenth birthday I graduated from Bad Axe High School. Buckley and Charlene hosted a party for me with an open bar. They provided plenty of beer, vodka, whiskey, and, of course, lots of Bucka's best wine for everyone, including my underage friends and me.

A few unlikely guests were invited. *My high school principal showed up!* My dad's boss, Mr. Paigne, and his family showed up. I didn't protest. They we're more guests with another envelope of cash.

When I received a card, I didn't collect them in a box, I took out the cash and threw the card away. Why did I need the damn card? To make a list of guests and send thank you notes? Why bother? I didn't even read them. I didn't care about their congratulatory notes and best wishes for my successful future. *I wanted the cash.*

Other than drinking a lot, the only memorable thing about the party was some strange advice Mr. Paigne gave me. He said, "I hear you're going to EMU. You better watch out for them jigaboos in Ypsilanti."

I didn't respond to his crass comment but thought to myself, *The only thing I need to worry about is rich, old white fuckers like you.*

After the party, I told Buckley about his boss's inappropriate comment and the old man said, "That Mr. Paigne is a real bitch bastard!"

I had managed to get accepted at a decent university because the previous fall Madge, with her vision always looking to the future, had helped me fill out an application to Eastern Michigan University. It was the only college application I had submitted. She also helped me write a great personal essay by telling me what topics, phrases, and words to use. Because of her kindness and forethought, I was able to get into a college and get the hell out of Bad Axe.

A couple of weeks after my party, my family was

at one of my cousin's graduation parties. Grandma Lucy had piled up a plate of Polish food and was heading to the basement to find a table. She stumbled and fell down the flight of stairs. She fell hard, but luckily, after tumbling down, she had a soft landing. My aunt was at the bottom of the stairs when Grandma fell.

She helped Lucy get to her feet and said, "It's a good thing those sacks of potatoes were there to catch you, ma!"

Old people falling down is never a good thing. It's usually an ominous sign that the end is near.

Grandma Kubacki died on the last day of June. Hundreds of people came to pay their respects and give condolences to the family. The whole mishpocheh, Grandma's friends from church, and old neighbors from back on the farm were all there. There were so many guests they couldn't all fit in the Zinger-Smigielski Funeral Home. There was a line out the door and down the front sidewalk. She also had an amazingly long funeral procession.

I was a pall bearer with seven of my cousins, we drove at the front of the procession. Looking back at the string of cars, I saw it was two and a half miles long. I shit you not! The funeral director ran out of orange flags for the vehicles. Grandma's funeral was joyful, tearful, and beautiful, but it was almost ruined by our parish priest.

Father Eoch didn't want to let an organist and choir from outside the parish play or sing at Lucy's funeral, and he did not want any part of a Polish Mass. Charlene, the woman who didn't care how people pronounced Kubacki (it's KOO-bot-skee, not KAH-bah-kee) and often said, “It’s my husband’s name, not mine, I don’t care how you pronounce it,” stood up for her Polish mother-in-law. Mom fought Father Eoch until he made concessions for the Polish Mass.

Muzey Polskie played the pipe organ and his choir from Parisville sang for Grandma’s funeral. They sang several hymns in Polish. I’m one hundred percent sure Grandma sang along with her crackling, slightly out of pitch, beautiful voice, watching over us somewhere in the church.

Later that summer, as Mass commentator, Mom added her own special prayer request during service alluding to Eoch’s non-priestly behavior before Grandma’s funeral. “May our priests and bishops be more Christ-like.” And the congregation replied, “Lord, hear our prayer.” Father gave Mom the hairy eyebrow when she offered her special ad-lib request. One of the parishioners noticed and asked Mom after church, “What’s up with you and Father Eoch, today?”

Near the end of summer, Gretchen and I went to an airshow at Bad Axe airport to see old biplanes, a World War II bomber, and aerial stunts. The Blue Angels made an appearance in their blue and gold Skyhawks. The jet squadron flew over and blew us away with their ear-piercing afterburners. It was awesome.

When we were waiting for the fighter jets to appear, I saw Madge’s mom in the crowd. Her old man, Josh, flew Cessnas and Pipers, so it wasn’t a surprise to see his wife there. Mr. Fleeting had promised to take Madge and I flying but he never did take us up.

"I see you, Irene."

"I see you too, Mr. Steve Kubacki."

My friends and I often teased Madge about her spiked-up, lacquered hair. Dion once said, "Her hair looks like a dandelion floating in the breeze."

The thought of it inspired me. I turned around and shouted to her, "Irene had a baby and her head popped off!"

She gave me a real stink eye. I grabbed Gretchen by the arm, we walked away, and blended in with the crowd.

Seeing Mrs. Fleeting got me thinking about Madge and all the good times we had parking on dusty back roads and farm fields. But she was gone. I harassed her whenever I saw her. Chased after her and her new boyfriend whenever I saw them riding through town on his fancy café racer. It would be impossible to get her back.

But I was bored with Gretchen and decided to call Maisie to see how she was doing. I didn't care that I had turned eighteen and she was now jailbait.

We talked for only a few minutes. I had never been inside her house, but while listening to her soft voice, I imagined Maisie sitting on a king-sized bed surrounded by big fluffy pillows. She spoke to me with kind, polite words, but made it clear that once a guy broke up with her, she would never take him back. Why the hell did I leave her alone that night? Why the hell didn't I go back and fuck her?

That fall, I was at EMU in Ypsilanti. Since I had registered late in the summer, the dorms were full and I had to rent an apartment off campus. *What terrible luck!* The challenge was finding someplace cheap. My buddy, Tony Marks, had completed two years at Eastern and was tired of living in the dorms. Franky Roberts had worked a factory gig for two years out of high school, was tired of the grind, and decided to attend EMU.

Marks, Roberts, and I got together and found a rundown apartment on the outskirts of campus. Besides junky furniture scrounged from home we had crappy mattresses provided by our landlord. We decorated our living room with a wall full of nude posters, some of the same centerfolds that had adorned the old tree fort wall. I skipped a lot of classes and blew off homework. I preferred sitting around drinking forty-ouncers of Goebel's and smoking the best pot from Ann Arbor. We always had some really good shit like the sinsemilla Zozecki had sold to us in Bad Axe.

I partied too much, my grades suffered, and I still wondered why. This didn't happen to me in high school. I partied almost every day back then and could still make passing grades. My loan money was running low, and ten dollars a gram for kind bud was tapping me out. There wasn't any cheap brown weed here like in Huron County. Only the good green, sticky stinky stuff. Tony and I talked about the weed situation and decided we had to do something about it.

We made a special trip to see Dion and his buddies

at MSU in East Lansing. We spent a whole day looking around the capital area trying to find a big bag of pot. After nearly twelve hours of poking around we scored a quarter pound of decent brown weed.

Marks and I thought it would be easy to unload sixteen quarter ounces baggies but it was nothing but a huge pain in the ass. We learned a couple of things in our dumb-ass business venture. Why was there no brown pot in Washtenaw County? Because, nobody wanted the shit. Every smoker wanted, and got, fluffy green sinsemilla *because it was everywhere.* Creative stoners had soilless hydroponic set ups in their attics, closets, and basements all over Ann Arbor. The second thing we learned was what to do when you can't sell a quarter pound of pot? Well, you smoke it yourself of course. We unloaded a few sacks to friends but smoked most of the QP ourselves in a few weeks.

At the end of my second year at Eastern, when everything was settling into place, Gretchen broke up with me for the third time. When I pleaded with her to stay, she wouldn't give in, yet thought it was a shame to break ties.

"We can still be friends can't we, Steve? Friendship lasts longer, anyway."

No way. I wasn't about to let that happen. I knew I could find somebody new in this crazy college town. Maybe even an awesome girl from Ann Arbor.

But I didn't have a chance. Girls from Ypsi and Ann Arbor were out of my league. I didn't know how to talk to them. What did a small-town hick like me have in common with these city girls? If only I knew someone from home that lived here. But there wasn't anyone that I knew of and I couldn't think of anyone to call back home, either.

Then I had a crazy thought. *It's fucking crazy. But maybe it was possible. Could I call Madge and get something going again? After all the shit I'd done?* Taunting her mom at the airport. Chasing her and her hot shot boyfriend. *With Madge? How?* Having zero prospects, I decided to look her up anyway, to see how she was doing. I knew she was going to school at Saginaw Valley. I called the campus operator and asked for Madge's number from the student directory.

I had seen Madge when I was still with Gretchen. We had bumped into each other at the Lewisville Bar over Christmas break. The place was known for good live rock music and serving underage patrons. Despite having *Under Twenty-one* stamped on their wrists in Day-Glo ink, almost anyone, especially young girls, could get booze in that place.

Gretchen had gone to the restroom. While she was occupied, I had a quick chat with Madge.

"Why aren't you here with your boyfriend?"

"I don't see him anymore."

"I heard he joined the Navy. Does that have anything to do with it?"

"No. I decided he's not my type."

"Oh, okay."

Gretchen was coming back from the bathroom and saw us talking. I quickly said goodbye, "It's been good catching up with you, Madge. I'll see you 'round."

It hadn't occurred to me that night at the club, but now that I had no chick, I was wondering what was Madge's type of guy. Maybe, she wanted a guy like me. After calling her at the dorms, I knew my hunch was right. Someone picked up the phone, I asked for Madge, and her roommate said, "Who's calling?" I told her, and despite being strangers, she handed over the phone and said, "*It's Steve.*" She already knew who I was.

Madge was packing to go home for the summer. She wanted to get a job waitressing somewhere in Huron County. Her dad was picking her up in an hour or so. She didn't have much time to talk but wanted to see me that weekend.

She said, "We should get together Saturday night."

"Okay, sounds good to me."

I picked her up, we went out drinking, parked in an old apple orchard, and had a real good time banging the hell out of each other.

One summer day shortly after my twenty-first birthday, we were talking about our huge families and realized we might be cousins. *What the fuck?* We studied the connections and figured out my aunt – dad's sister – had married Madge's dad's cousin. We had no direct blood relation, thank God!

That fall Madge transferred to EMU. Marks had moved back to Bad Axe, and Roberts and I wanted a bigger place, so we found a two-bedroom townhouse for him, Madge and me.

Despite being Catholic, Irene and Josh helped us out. They gave us a small Formica dining table and three chairs they had used as newlyweds. Irene gave Madge two house plants from her collection, a huge jade tree and an even bigger split-leaf philodendron, for our apartment. She even loaned us her rusty Chevy truck and filled it up with gas. We finished packing Madge's things at the farm and went into Bad Axe to pick up my stuff.

I backed Irene's truck onto the lawn to the front porch. After I loaded my things, Mom gave me a hug and a kiss. Dad squeezed the guts right out of me, handed me a twenty, and said, "You'll need this for gas."

Madge hopped in the truck and waited.

"You know we don't approve of this Steve?"

"We don't know," Mom said, "if this is the right thing to do."

They had already said, several times, that we'd be living in sin.

"Well, I don't care what you think. We love each other. We're adults and can make our own decisions. We'll get married and buy a house after college."

"Oh, Steve."

"Stephen Mark."

I stormed off the front porch and got inside the truck. I yelled, "We don't care what you think, we don't care what your church thinks, and we don't care what your God thinks. We're going to live in sin. We're shacking up!"

I slammed the door, drove off the lawn, and cruised down South Street.

A couple of weeks later, I had settled into a more-or-less domestic routine at our apartment. I was doing better at school. Pulling decent grades. Had a part-time job at a tobacco shop, was selling my plasma a few times a week, and quit pulling shoplifting scams. Wasn't drinking much, I still smoked a lot of weed, but had quit all the other drugs. So, you know, when the good sinsemilla in Ann Arbor ran dry, I had to find some weed, somewhere, fast.

Madge and I were in Huron County to visit for the weekend and pick up a few things for our new place. While in town, I wanted to score some pot.

I drove to Rizzo's place. He was renting a little house, shacked up with his girlfriend. He answered the door wearing black jeans and no shirt. I went inside.

"You mean it's dry up here too?"

"Yeah, Kubacki. There's been nothing here for a month."

"Come on, Hendricks, you've always got pot. You don't have a bud stashed somewhere?"

"Nope. I don't have any weed."

"You don't even have any roaches?"

"Well, yeah. I always have some roaches. But that's all I got. I'm saving them for later."

He went in the bedroom to put on a shirt. I looked down and saw some roaches in the ashtray. I picked one up, carefully pinched it between my fingers, lit it up, and started puffing. He came out from his bedroom.

"Don't smoke my fucking roaches. That's all I fucking got, man!"

"What's the big fucking deal, Hendricks? It's only a roach."

"You fucking asshole!"

He went into the bedroom again and came out with a .22 pointed in my face.

"What the fuck are you doing Rizzo?"

"I told you not to smoke my fucking roaches, Kubacki."

His girlfriend came into the room, convinced Rizzo not to shoot me, and I got the hell out of there.

Not sure why I did it, I hated talking to the police for any reason, but I drove to city hall and talked to the desk clerk.

"Officer Valentine's on duty if you'd like to talk to him. You tell him what happened and maybe he can file a complaint. He's in his office now."

I told Valentine what happened. He said he'd check it out. After I filed the complaint, he handed me his card and said to call him tomorrow. I told him I would be back in Ypsilanti because I had classes at Eastern.

"You don't have to be in town. Call me from school."

I called Valentine the next day.

"Mr. Kubacki, there's definitely enough evidence for you to press charges. I spoke to Mr. Hendricks and his girlfriend. She's a credible witness. I can go ahead and press charges if you'd like."

"Officer Valentine?"

"Yes, Mr. Kubacki."

"I don't want to press charges."

"Oh? But why not Mr. Kubacki?"

I said, "I just don't want to. I've changed my mind," and ended the call.

Valentine didn't press charges against Hendricks either. *He gave him a pass.* Many people in my small town were gracious and often let things slide, sometimes when intervention would have been better. I couldn't forgive Rizzo for what he'd done. It would be decades before I forgave *anyone,* and when I was ready for forgiveness, the most difficult, and last person I forgave was *myself.*

But on that day, when I hung up the phone, I just wanted to leave Rizzo alone. I wanted him to leave me alone. Why did I ever hang out with Hendricks? *I wasn't anything like him.* He was crazy. Everyone knew he was crazy. The kid was fucked-up. He was a bad seed. A lemon.

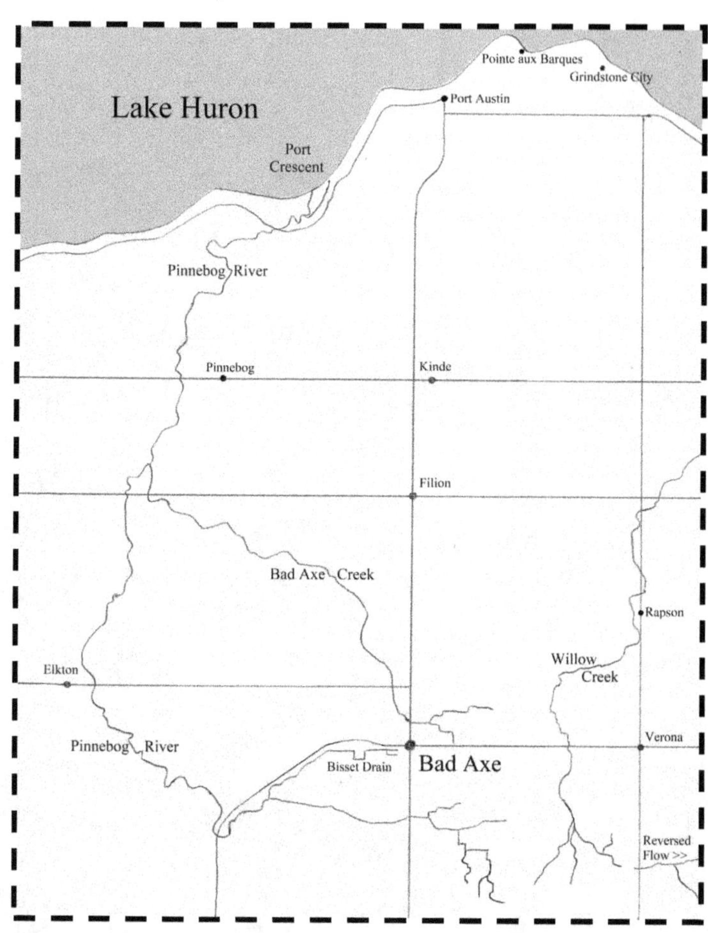
Lake Huron
Pointe aux Barques
Grindstone City
Port Austin
Port
Crescent
Pinnebog River
Pinnebog
Kinde
Filion
Bad Axe Creek
Rapson
Willow
Creek
Elkton
Verona
Pinnebog River
Bisset Drain
Bad Axe
Reversed
Flow >>

www.ingramcontent.com/pod-product-compliance
Lightning Source LLC
LaVergne TN
LVHW050613100826
845148LV00011B/1571

* 9 7 9 8 2 1 8 7 3 2 7 0 7 *